CW00404884

Preface

The objective of this book is to give an insight into Android programming based on practical app projects. The apps have different objectives and target groups and hence one can extend and develop them further based on his/her Android knowledge. Thanks to active programming, the users will be quickly acquainted with the work environment and will learn how to solve problems in Android step-by-step. Android Studio, which is a completely new development environment, will be used for programming.

TARGET GROUP OF THIS BOOK

This book is intended for everyone who is interested in the Android app development and would like to learn the same with DIY examples.

REQUIREMENTS FOR THE COMPUTER

What are the requirements for the computer? You can select any modern operating system of your choice (Windows XP, Windows 7/8, Mac OS X and Linux). You will need Administrator rights for installation.

ANDROID TELEPHONE OR TABLET

Since an emulator is integrated in Android Studio, you can start Android development even without an Android telephone or a tablet. Testing with the emulator makes sense since the app can be tested with all possible Android versions, screen sizes and resolutions. In addition, you can also use specific debugging options in the emulator such as Hierarchy View which can otherwise be used only with a Google developer telephone. However, the emulator has its limitations. For example: One cannot make telephone calls, the options to test the GPS are restricted, the accelerator in the telephone responds to movements; one cannot hold the emulator in hand, which makes it difficult or even impossible to test the games.

If you are not well-versed with an Android device until now, you might ask which would be an ideal choice from a developer's point of view.

I have given a few pointers here, which will hopefully make the decision making easier.

Which Android version should the telephone use? The latest? Probably yes, when you are thinking of developing an app for the latest version of Android. If you want to develop apps for the masses, you must know the Android versions used by the masses. Based on a test conducted by Google at the end of August 2014, the distribution is as follows:

- Android 2.2 Froyo API 8 => 0.7%

- Android 2.3.3 - 2.3.7 Gingerbread API 10 => 13.6%
- Android 3.2 Honeycomb API 13 => 0.1%
- Android 4.0.3 - 4.0.4 Ice Cream Sandwich API 15 => 10.6%
- Android 4.1.x Jelly Bean API 16 => 26.5%
- Android 4.2.x Jelly Bean API 17 => 19.8%
- Android 4.3 Jelly Bean API 18 => 7.9%

    Android 4.4 KitKat API 19 => 20.9%

This means that Android 4.x versions are used by than 70% users. Since Android Version 4.4 KitKat has been released, this statistics will soon further improve in favour of Android 4.x and probably get worse for Froyo and Gingerbread.

Screen size and resolution are other factors that can influence the purchase of a developer device. Testing the layout of an app is extremely important. You can imagine that nobody would like an app where the text is not legible or the buttons are too small and one always accidentally clicks on 3 other things when one wants to click on "Next". My tip: search for the most commonly used screen resolutions in Google. In October 2013, the vast majority of devices had a resolution of 480x800 pixels.

For the latest information, visit:

http://developer.android.com/about/dashboards/index.html

JAVA KNOWLEDGE

Knowledge of Java is recommended. However, you can also start with this book and refer to a Java book wherever you face problems due to the lack of Java knowledge. A list of free Java books that are used in schools, colleges and universities is given in the annexe.

HOW THIS BOOK IS STRUCTURED?

This book has 3 parts:

Part 1:

The first part deals with the installation and configuration of Java and Android Studio. You will get an overview of the development environment and an insight how the project structure of an Android app looks in Android Studio.

The 1st part concludes with the creation and commissioning of a test app project. This will ensure that Android Studio functions as expected. You would not appreciate if you realise some parts are missing when you are already in the middle of a book, would you?

Part 2:

The second parts deals with the creation of different app projects.

Each of the apps begins with a plan. The practical implementation of the app idea is then explained.

Among other things, you will learn the following on the course of completing the apps:

Creating different screen layouts

Supporting different screen sizes

Designing clickable buttons and assigning functions to them

Using and managing the resources

Creating a series of different activities

Creating a database

Adding an ActionBar

Creating animation

Making calculations in the app

Using Google libraries

Working with Google maps

Integrating ads in the app

Providing support for different languages

Preparing the app for the Android market

Complete source code is provided for each app project; refer to the links.

Part 3:

Advanced sections are included in the third part. These include:

Gradle

Connecting your project with Github

Product Flavours - Build Types - Build Variants

GameEngines AndEngine and libGDXLinks for the source code and more information is given in the annexe.

About Android Studio

In May 2013, Google presented the new development environment for Android apps during the developers' conference. The new IDE is intended to replace Eclipse and is based on the "IntelliJ IDEA" Java-IDE by JetBrains.

The powerful Code-Editor with built-in functions such as "Smart Editing", which ensures better legible code, or "Advanced Code Refactoring" is one of the core components of Android Studio.

The Gradle Build System is another novel feature introduced with Android Studio. It replaces the Ant Build System used until now.

Gradle allows developers to create various configurations so that different app versions can be produced using the same code. This is really useful when you want to release a free and a paid version of an app.

Gradle improves the reusability of the code and the integration on a build server.

Similar to Eclipse, the layout of an app can be created either in the text editor or in a graphical interface (design mode) in Android Studio.

The design mode was further improved for Android Studio. The app layout shows the layout for different resolutions, Android versions and country-specific special features in the preview.

A series of new features and services were integrated in Android Studio. The developer console gives developers tips for optimising an app and it also allows uploading the "string files" (strings.xml) to be translated to a central server, and to insert them again in the app after translating them.

Android Studio was also enhanced with an option to add Google Cloud Messaging (CGM) to the project that allows sending messages to the app and receiving the messages from the app on the cloud server.

It is not a new feature to connect an Android app with a cloud server/ App Engine Server app. The integration into an Android app project is the novelty. Earlier, it was essential to create an App Engine Server app and an Android app that is supposed to work with this server app separately from each other.

Knowledge to create an App Engine Server app using Java is essential for using the GCM. This is not explained in this book.

Here are the links of two starter websites for interested users:

- https://developers.google.com/appengine/docs/java/
- http://android-developers.blogspot.se/2013/06/adding-backend-to-your-app-in-android.html

Android Studio has been developed by Google in collaboration with JetBrains and is based on the community version of IntelliJ. JetBrains Java IDE InelliJ supports Android app development since 2 years. Current IntelliJ Version 12 has new features that have been developed in collaboration with Google, but not yet integrated. These will be integrated in Version 13+. Like before, even the new version will support a series of development environments such as Java, Android, Adobe Gaming SDK, Groovy, Scala.

On the other hand, Android Studio will be restricted to the development of Android apps. Google has not specified an official release date for Android Studio.

Android Studio is still being developed and should not be used in the productive app development as yet. However, since a major part of the IDE is already functional, users can still start befriending Android Studio. This is recommended since they can rev up once the finished version is released.

You can download the current version of Android Studios from the following link:

http://developer.android.com/sdk/installing/studio.html

Introduction

Those, who want to start with Android app programming, must simultaneously fight on two fronts. Not only they have to deal with Android programming, but must also learn a new development environment. Naturally, this fact has been taken into account in this book. All projects are exclusively created in Android Studio and individual steps for Android Studio are explained while developing these projects. In addition, this book also has a chapter "Overview of the IDE" which contains a tour through the most important menus of Android Studio. A few decisive changes concerning the development of Android apps were simultaneously made with the introduction of Android Studio. A series of these changes are applicable for the new Gradle Build System. In the sample projects, Gradle is dealt with only to the extent required for the project. A separate chapter named Gradle is included; it contains more information about Gradle and its operation and significance.

CONSTITUENTS OF AN APP

The app normally comprises a series of different files that can be classified into 4 categories:

- Java classes
- Layout files
- Resources
- Configuration files

We assume that our app two screens - the first shows a list from which individual elements can be clicked and the second shows the result after clicking the element. The app would look as shown below:

First screen

After starting the app, a Java file is first started. This Java file contains the file name of the layout file that needs to be displayed and starts it as a so-called view, where we can see the list on the screen. The layout file contains the design structure (list) and information regarding texts and images that need to be displayed. Texts and images are stored in the resource folders and files. The layout file contains only the links to the resources. The functioning of a layout file is similar to that of a website (HTML).

The Java file started (activity) not only has the function of displaying the fist screen, but it also waits for an event wherein an element from the list is clicked. It reacts to the click and guides the app to the second Java file.

The second screen that would be shown after clicking the 3rd element from the list

A separate layout file is allocated to the second Java file, which is also an activity; the second Java file shows this layout file. The functionality for this app is thus utilised.

In general, we can say that we need an activity and the associated layout file to display something on the screen. However, not all Java files, which are sometimes a part of an app, comprise activities. This means that not all Java classes display something on the screen. Adapter and databases are other commonly used Java classes. All three types of Java classes are used in different projects mentioned in this book.

Android Studio is used as the primary tool for developing the apps in this book.

INSTALLING JAVA AND ANDROID STUDIO

If Java SDK and Android Studio have already been installed, you can continue with the "First project" chapter to test the work environment.

If not, a step-by-step guide is given below.

In principle, 3 things are required for the Android development:

- Java SDK

- Android SDK

- An environment for building the apps

You can download the Java SDK for your operating system from Oracle's homepage. The Android SDK is included in Android Studio and need not be separately installed. Eclipse, IntelliJ and Android Studio are normally available as the IDE/ integrated development environment.

Eclipse and IntelliJ, up to version 12, work with the Ant Build System which will no longer be supported 100% by Google.

The Android Studio development environment uses the Gradle Build System to test and build apps.

The new Android Studio development environment is exclusively used in this book.

Java installation

Go to Oracle's download page

http://www.oracle.com/technetwork/java/javase/downloads/index.html

click on <JDK download> and then on the latest Java Development Kit on the next page, e.g.

> *Java SE Development Kit 7u40*

When you have decided for a Java version, download the corresponding file depending on your operating system and install it.

Windows users are recommended to set the path for JAVA_HOME as follows:

In the control panel

-> System -> Advanced System Settings -> Advanced -> Environment variable

Click on *New* and generate a value for the Java environmental variable:

Name: JAVA_HOME

Value: e.g. C:Files.7.0_40

If CLASSPATH does not exist yet, create it afresh and enter the value depending on the path: C:Files.7.0_40Under PATH, specify the path depending on the value:

> *;C:Files.7.0_40*

Testing the Java installation

Enter the following command in the terminal window:

```
java -version
```

This will show an active Java version, e.g.:

```
java version "1.6.0_37"
Java(TM) SE Runtime Environment (build 1.6.0_37-b06-434-11M3909)
Java HotSpot(TM) 64-Bit Server VM (build 20.12-b01-434, mixed mode)
```

Installing Android Studio

Pre-installed and usable Java 1.6 or 1.7 by Oracle is a prerequisite. Android Studio functions better with Java 1.6 in many cases.

Download the installation package from here depending on the operating system used:

http://developer.android.com/sdk/installing/studio.html

Specifically for Windows:

Double-click the downloaded EXE file and follow the instructions.

Specifically for Mac OS:

The installation of Android Studio requires the following system setting:

In System Preferences, go to Security and Privacy, and select *Anywhere* under "Allow applications downloaded from" option.

Then double-click the downloaded DMG file. Then drag the application icon in the programme folder.

Specifically for Linux:

Unpack the downloaded TGZ file and then copy the folders to the desired location.

Start Android Studio using the *studio.sh* file that is located in the *android-studio/bin/* folder.

Android Studio comes out of the box ready to use. However, starting the SDK Manager and downloading and installing a few additional packages is recommended to be able to use its entire scope right from the beginning.

You can use the SDK Manager to install and update Android platforms, support libraries and Android development tools.

Since Android is being continuously developed, you must regularly check for updates that could be important for your own app development

Android SDK Manager

You can start the SDK Manager using three different methods:

From Welcome screen -> Configure -> SDK Manager

Use the icon in the menu bar

and via

Tools → Android → SDK Manager

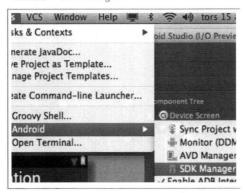

Use a check mark to select the desired SDK platforms /Android versions and tools. Then click on

      <Install .. packages..>.

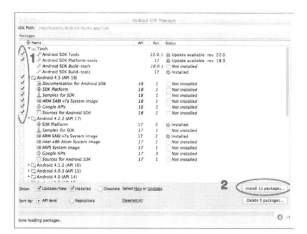

Accept the licence with "Accept Licence" and press <Install> to start the download and installation process.

You should install the following packages as described above if they are not yet installed:

Tools required:

    Android SDK tools

    Android SDK platform tools

    Android SDK build-tools (at least one, preferably the latest)

    Android Version

At least one Android version must have been installed. After installation, the current Android version must appear in Android Studio, e.g.:

Android 4.4 API 19 or higher

At least the SDK platform package for an Android version is required. If you want to run the app on the emulator, you must install at least the **ARM EABI** v7a System Image. If you have an Intel-based computer, you should also install the Intel x86 Atom System Image since it is slightly faster.

Extras required:

Android Support Repository

Android Support Library

Google Play services

Google Repository

UBS driver (Windows) for Google telephones

First project

This chapter describes the process to create an Android project in Android Studio. For this, you need to use a template provided in Android Studio. This template is called a "Blank template" and it creates a fully operational "Hello World" app.

You do not require any programming knowledge to create this project. You simply need to test the working environment. You need to check whether Android Studio can build an app and run it on an emulator or an Android telephone.

This is also a good opportunity to view the project structure of a project created in Android Studio and to get well-versed with the working environment.

Creating a new project

When open Android Studio for the first time after installing it, you will see a Welcome screen containing various selection options in the Quick Start menu.From the Quick Start menu, select "New Project"; you will be guided through multiple screens to create the new project.

The "New Project" input screen will then be displayed.

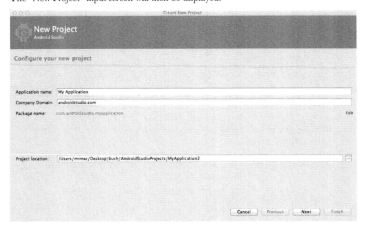

Application name:

The name of the app that should later appear in the application, e.g. in the title bar or in Google Play Store.

You can select this name freely. The strings entered here are stored in the "app_name" variable in the "strings.xml" file and can be edited in this file if required. (Spaces are allowed)

Module name:

Rule - no spaces

Package name:

It is the "identification name" of the app. It is included in all Java files and in the AndroidManifest.xml file.

Project location:

The location where the current project is stored on the hard disk. It can be changed if required.

Minimum required SDK:

API 7, Android 2.1 is preset here by default. You can select a higher API/ Android version in many cases. For example, all Ads providers such as Google's Admob require the Android version API 8 as the minimum requirement.

Click on <Next> to select the app template: When you select the Blank Activity template, a "Hello World" app will be created automatically.

Click on <Next> again to open the view for the "Activity Name" and "Layout Name", i.e. the name of the first activity to be generated and the corresponding layout file.

Now it's time to click on "Finish" to build the project structure using the selected template. In our case, the "Blank Template" generates the structure of the "Hello World" app as shown below.

The files marked with a red rectangle are the project files that we will edited.

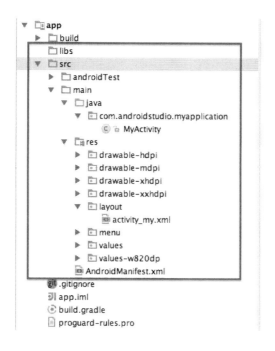

The icon for the app

Your App project comes by default with a standard Android Icon. The App icon can be customized using the Image Asset.

Right-click on the "app" directory of your project, choose "New" than "Image Asset".

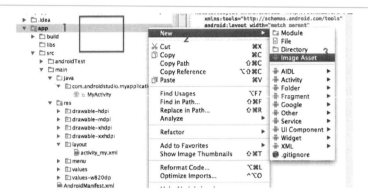

Here you can upload an image/clip art or enter text that should bear the app icon. If you select the clip art and text, you also need to select the foreground and background colours.

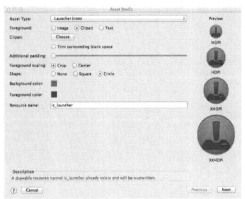

Project structure

The users, who have created Android projects using Eclipse, will realise that the project structure looks different than that in Eclipse or even IntelliJ up to version 12.

As shown in the above screenshot, almost all project files are now located in the src/ directory along with the resources and the AndroidManifest file.

In addition, the build.gradle file and the proguard-rules.txt file are located outside the src/ directory, but are in the root directory of the project.

The new project structure is generated through the conversion to a Gradle-based build system. This structure ensures more flexibility for the build process and allows creating multiple build variants from the same code.

The build.gradle file is a configuration file that controls the build process. We will edit this in the course of creating an app. Explanations for individual configuration entries will be added when these are used.

A rough overview of Gradle is given in the annexe under Gradle.

Which files are stored in the project structure, and where?

The directory has a directory called src/ where all resource files are stored. Files of the main project are stored in the main/ sub-directory. One app can comprise multiple sub-projects. Resources of these projects are stored in their separate folders having the same structure as that of main/.

The main/ source folder has 2 sub-directories, java/ and res/

| -- main | -- src | -- res

The src/ directory contains all Java files.

All resource files are stored in the res/ directory. Resource files are sub-divided into categories that have their separate folders.

res/ | -- drawable-hdpi | -- drawable-mdpi | -- drawable-xdpi | -- drawable-xxdpi | -- layout | -- layout-land | -- menu | -- values | -- values-w820dp

Images are stored in the drawable folders. These four different folders represent different screen resolutions and screen sizes. For a list of currently supported sizes, visit:

http://developer.android.com/design/style/devices-displays.html

The layout/ folder contains all layout files that show the content on the screen. You can optionally use the layout-land/ folder if you want to create a customised layout for the landscape mode.

The menu/ directory contains one or more configuration files for menu items such as "Settings" in the ActionBar.

The values/ folder contains three files: dimens.xml, strings.xml and styles.xml

The dimens.xml files contains screen specifications for distances or font sizes

The strings.xml file contains all texts that should be displayed in the app.

The values/ folder contains texts for the default language. If additional languages are supported, you must create the new values/ folder, which contains the strings.xml file for the new language, for every new language.

Example:

English is the default language for the app -> the strings.xml file in the values/ folder contains text in English. German should be supported as an additional language. The folder for German is called values-de/ and it has a separate strings.xml containing all texts in German.

The styles.xml file contains definitions for the theme of the app.

You can optionally use the values-w820dp/ directory if you want to create app layouts for tablets.

If you require additional folders in the course of the app creation, you can create them manually.

THE HELLO WORLD APP

The Hello World app, that we have created more or less automatically, is a completely operational app.

If you click on <Design> in the editor, you can see the structure of the app layout.

The app layout is defined in an xml file. You will need an activity (Java file) to display the layout file on the screen. This was automatically created for us.

The created Java files looks as shown below and has 6 parts in this case:

```
package com.greendog.example.myapplication.app;
import android.support.v7.app.ActionBarActivity;
import android.os.Bundle;
import android.view.Menu;
import android.view.MenuItem;
public class MainActivity extends ActionBarActivity {
    @Override
    protected void onCreate(Bundle savedInstanceState) {
        super.onCreate(savedInstanceState);
        setContentView(R.layout.activity_main);
    }
    @Override
    public boolean onCreateOptionsMenu(Menu menu) {
// Inflate the menu; this adds items to the action bar if it is present.
        getMenuInflater().inflate(R.menu.main, menu);
        return true;
    }
    @Override
    public boolean onOptionsItemSelected(MenuItem item) {
        // Handle action bar item clicks here. The action bar will
        // automatically handle clicks on the Home/Up button, so long
        // as you specify a parent activity in AndroidManifest.xml.
        int id = item.getItemId();
        if (id == R.id.action_settings) {
            return true;
        }
        return super.onOptionsItemSelected(item);
    }
}
```

The first part:

The first row in a Java class is always the packet name.

```
package com.greendog.example.myapplication.app;
```

The second part:

It contains all import definitions.

```
import android.support.v7.app.ActionBarActivity;
import android.os.Bundle;
import android.view.Menu;
import android.view.MenuItem;
```

The third part:

The new class and the class type are defined. This is an activity that is capable of integrating an ActionBar.

```
public class MainActivity extends ActionBarActivity {
```

The fourth part:

The activity is started in the onCreate method and the associated layout is shown on the screen.

```
@Override
    protected void onCreate(Bundle savedInstanceState) {
        super.onCreate(savedInstanceState);
        setContentView(R.layout.activity_main);
    }
```

The fifth part:

The Options menu is provided. It retrieves its information from the res/menu/main.xml file. When the app is running, the Options menu can be accessed from the ActionBar or from the Menu key of the telephone.

```
@Override
    public boolean onCreateOptionsMenu(Menu menu) {
// Inflate the menu; this adds items to the action bar if it is present.
        getMenuInflater().inflate(R.menu.main, menu);
        return true;
    }
```

The sixth part:

You can now click individual elements of the Options menu. Parts for the Options menu do not have the correct function as yet. They are only a placeholder at present.

```
@Override
    public boolean onOptionsItemSelected(MenuItem item) {
        // Handle action bar item clicks here. The action bar will
        // automatically handle clicks on the Home/Up button, so long
        // as you specify a parent activity in AndroidManifest.xml.
        int id = item.getItemId();
        if (id == R.id.action_settings) {
            return true;
        }
        return super.onOptionsItemSelected(item);
    }
```

Adding the ActionBar to the app

In order to add an ActionBar in the project, you need to edit the AndroidManifest.xml file from the /src/main/ directory and the main.xml file from the /res/menu/ directory.

First open the AndroidManifest.xml file and add a row for the theme.

```
<activity    android:name="com.greendog.example.myapplication.MainActivity"
             android:label="@string/app_name"
             android:theme="@style/Theme.AppCompat.Light" >
```

Save the changes and close the file.

Adding a button to the ActionBar

You can link the icons for the ActionBar either from the sdk associated with Android Studio or copy them physically in the drawable folder. If you want to support very old Android versions with your app, we recommend downloading the icons as a pack and copy in the folder.

If you use the icon pack and copied icons in your drawable folder, the code for the icon is:

```
android:icon="@drawable/ic_action_search"
```

The reference for an icon from the sdk is:

```
android:icon="@android:drawable/ic_action_search"
```

You can download the ActionBar icon pack from:

http://developer.android.com/design/downloads/index.html#action-bar-icon-pack

In order to add menu items, open the main.xml file from the /res/menu/ directory and add or modify:

```
<?xml version="1.0" encoding="utf-8"?>
<menu xmlns:android="http://schemas.android.com/apk/res/android"
    xmlns:greendog="http://schemas.android.com/apk/res-auto >
    <item
        android:id="@+id/action_about"
        android:title="@string/action_about"
        android:icon="@android:drawable/ic_dialog_info"
        greendog:showAsAction="always" />
    <item
        android:id="@+id/action_settings"
        android:title="@string/action_settings"
        android:icon="@android:drawable/ic_menu_preferences"
        greendog:showAsAction="ifRoom" />
</menu>
```

The v7 appcompat support library cannot use "android" as "namespace". I have used greendog as my "namespace" in the example. You can select any name that you like. The main.xml file shows the approximate result of the future ActionBar in the preview. Pages, which can invoke the menu, will be developed later for the both menu items, namely Info and Settings.

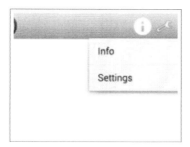

The app is complete and operational as is was created. We can now run the app either in an emulator or on an Android device.

Adding comments

COMMENTS IN JAVA FILES

Comments of "single-line" and "multi-line" types can be included in Java files. Single-line comments

Single-line comments can be normal text to include a description/explanation. However, they can also include code that the user does not want to use temporarily, but does not want to delete it either.

// This is a single-line comment

Example:

```
public boolean onCreateOptionsMenu(Menu menu) {
 // Inflate the menu; this adds items to the action bar if it is present.
        getMenuInflater().inflate(R.menu.main, menu);
```

Single-line comments can also be included after the code.

Example:

```
getMenuInflater().inflate(R.menu.main, menu); // the main.xml file in the
menu folder
```

Multi-line comments can be normal text to include a description/explanation. However, they can also include code that the user does not want to use temporarily, but does not want to delete it either. /*   This is a multi-line comment   included by Barbara Hohensee */

Android Studio contains a menu to convert single or multi-line text/code into comments.

Code -> Comment with Line Comment Code -> Comment with Block Comment In order to use one of these menus, select you text/code with the mouse and then select a menu item. If you want to reactivate the commented code later, i.e. if you want to revoke the commenting, select the section again and select the corresponding menu.

Comments in Android XML files

The tags for single and multi-line comments are identical.   <!-- This is a single-line comment --> <!-- Multi-line comment included by Barbara Hohenee -->   The menu for converting the selected text/code   Code -> Comment with Line Comment Code -> Comment with Block Comment can be used here.

Setting up the emulators

Installing the default emulator from the Android SDK

Emulators are often abbreviated as AVD (Android Virtual Devices)

In Android Studio and the opened Android project, either click on the "AVD Manager" icon

or Tools → Android → AVD Manager

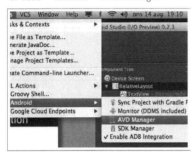

The "Android Virtual Device Manager" window will then open.

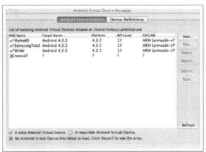

Here you can set up new emulators, and edit, repair or delete existing ones.

You can also directly start an emulator selected from the list.

Apart from this, you can start an emulator from <Run>. See "Run and Build Configuration" for more info.

The list of emulators contain three icons that indicate the status of the emulator:

The green check mark indicates that the emulator has been installed correctly and can be used for executing corresponding Android projects.

The "broken" icon indicates that the emulator was installed, but can be used only after a repair.

The red cross indicates that the emulator is defective or originates from an earlier development environment such as Eclipse or IntelliJ up to Version 12. Since these emulators do not affect Android Studio, they can remain here without any problem. You can retain them if you want to simultaneously work with Eclipse or IntelliJ up to Version 12.

SETTING UP NEW EMULATORS

Select <New..> to start the set up and open an additional window named "Create new Android Virtual Devices".

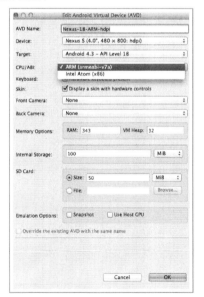

You can select <Edit> to return to this configuration window and change settings any number of times.

AVD Name:

You can select this name freely; spaces are not allowed. This name will be later included in the list of emulators.

Device:

Here you can select one of the prepared emulator configurations.

Target:

The option available in "Target" depends on Android versions that have been installed using SDK Manager.

CPU/ ABI:

Here you can select either Intel or ARM Image depending on what you have installed before via SDK Manager.

You can adapt other settings like front camera or SD card simulation as per the test requirements if the same is relevant for the app.

After you press <OK>, a results window will be shown; the created emulator is now equipped.

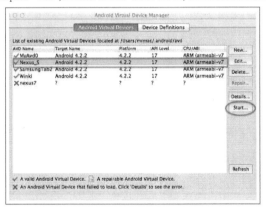

When you press <Start..>, the "Launch Option" window will be opened; if necessary, you can change the default resolution and size of the emulator. A little bit of trial and error will not harm anything. You can also change these settings whenever you start the emulator. Then, confirm the settings with <OK> and wait for the start of emulator patiently. Isn't it a time for another coffee break?

Once the emulator is installed completely, you can click on the green triangle (Run) in the toolbar to run the app on the emulator.

The emulator displays the emulator port and emulator name in the top bar.

5554:KitKat displayed here means that the port of the emulator is 5554 and the name of emulator is KitKat.

Port number 5554 is automatically allocated to the emulator called first; the second has post number 5556, the third 5558, etc. A maximum of 16 emulators can be opened simultaneously.

You can communicate with the emulator via the port number from another emulator or via Telnet.

If you have opened two emulators, they can send SMSs.

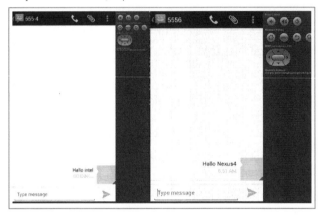

You have more options to communicate with the emulator via Telnet.

The Telnet commend is called from a terminal window (Linux, Mac) or a CMD window (Windows). If you are using Windows 8, Telnet is disabled by default. Proceed as follows to enable Telnet in Windows 8:

1.   Open "Control Panel"

2.   Click on "Programs"

3.   Click on "Enable or Disable Windows Features"

A small window will open, wherein you can enable or disable (depending on your wish) "Telnet Client" and/or "Telnet Server".Select or deselect the desired checkbox and press "OK".

Wait for a short while until Telnet is enabled. You need to restart your system.

Now open either CMD or the terminal window. Use the following command to establish a contact with the first emulator whose port number is 5554.

```
telnet localhost 5554
```

Use the following command to send an SMS to the emulator as shown in the following screenshot:

```
sms send 7575 How are you?
```

Here is a practical example if you want to use the Telnet communication option for testing an app:

When an app is running, it is on the foreground. For example, when a call comes when an application is running, the desired action is to switch the app in the background; this means although the app is not visible to the user, it is not closed. After the user accepts the call, talks with the other caller and finally completes the conversation, our app should again come in the foreground and continue as intended.

You can use the following command to simulate an incoming call from telephone number 0316114287:

```
gsm call 0316114287
```

You can view other commands by entering 'help'.

Shortcut key for the emulator

<CTRL> <F11> is probably one of the most important shortcut keys and toggles between the portrait and landscape formats. For more shortcut keys and helpful information, visit

http://developer.android.com/tools/help/emulator.html

Installing and setting up an external emulator

Genymotion

The emulator that you have just set up is included in the Android SDK. Another emulator named genymotion can also work with Android Studio. Since the emulator has nothing to do with the Android SDK and Google, a module of the genymotion developer is used for the set up. genymotion has one free version and two other versions that can be purchased via an annual licence.

Among other things, the genymotion emulator is characterised by its speed and emulation of sensors.

The genymotion emulator runs in VirtualBox. If the VirtualBox programme is not installed on your computer, start with installing the same.

Step 1:

You can download VirtualBox from:

https://www.virtualbox.org/wiki/Downloads

When installing VirtualBox, accept the default values and restart the computer after completing the installation.

Step 2:

Create an account on www.genymotion.com. Then download the installation package depending on your operating system.

VirtualBox is included in the installation package for Windows. Linux and Mac OS users must install VirtualBox separately.

Step 3:

Install the genymotion installation package.

Step 4:

Start genymotion -> create a new virtual device

Step 5:

Specify the complete path of the Android SDK in settings.

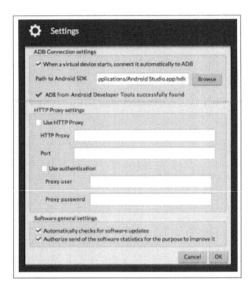

Step 6:

Now click on <PLAY> to start the emulator.

If you get an error message when using Mac, you can try starting the emulator from the command line using one of the following commands:

```
sudo /Library/StartupItems/VirtualBox/VirtualBox restart
```

or

```
sudo /Library/ApplicationSupport/VirtualBox/LaunchDaemons/VirtualBoxStartup.sh restart
```

The Mac OS shows 'permission issues' in some cases. In such a case, go to the Disk Utility app and start "Repair Disk Permissions".

Step 7:

Download the IntelliJ IDEA plugin from Genymotion's website.

Step 8:

Open Android Studio

From the Welcome screen, select:

- Configure
- Plugins
- Install plugin from disk

and navigate to the downloaded IDEA plugin.

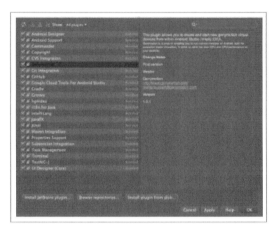

Step 9:

Restart Android Studio

Step 10:

Now select any project that you want to run in the genymotion emulator. After the project is completely loaded, click on the Run icon and select the genymotion emulator from the "choose device" window.

Alternatively, you can also start the genymotion emulator using the new genymotion icon in the toolbar.

If new versions are available, these are shown and you can upgrade the emulator from Android Studio.

Other emulators are sometimes included in external SDKs. For example, this is the case with the SDK of Samsung Gear that has been used for developing Samsung's Android smartwatch Gear:

http://developer.samsung.com/samsung-gear

Connecting a telephone of a tablet

If you want to run the app on an actual telephone or Android tablet, you need to change a setting in the device and ensure that the corresponding USB driver is installed.

Setting in the device, telephone or tablet

Menu - Settings -> Developer Options -> Enable USB Debugging

USB driver

Mac users need not install a driver. The same is also applicable to most Linux distributions.

Linux users can visit the following website to get valuable information about USB drivers.

http://developer.android.com/tools/device.html

Windows users can refer to the following website for information regarding OEM drivers of various manufacturers and regarding installation itself:

http://developer.android.com/tools/extras/oem-usb.html

Connecting the device with Android Studio

Now connect the Android device with the computer using a USB cable.

Once you click on Run (green triangle), you should be able to see the connected telephone or tablet, in addition to the emulator, in the "Choose device" menu.

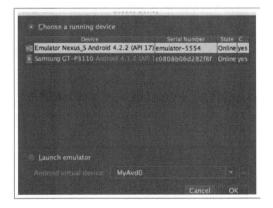

Select the telephone or the tablet and click on <OK>. Now you can enjoy the Hello World app on your telephone or tablet. However, you cannot do much with this app. This app can only display the "Hello World!" text on the screen.

The Run command triggers Android Studio to search the code for errors, to build the code and pack it into an APK (app package). This APK is copied on the device after selecting an emulator or a device.In the next step, the app is opened with the first activity of the project. An activity is always associated with a layout file. This layout file is called by the activity and its contents are shown on the screen.

Building and running the app

In order to run the app, you simply need to click on the green triangle icon or use the Run menu command. Android Studio will first compile the code and then makes it available for running.

Gradle compiles the code and you can monitor the progress in the status bar at the bottom of the screen.

If there are error messages due to problems in the code, a log window is shown in the lower part of the screen.

When the code is ready to run on a device, the "choose device" window will open. In the top list, you can see the emulators that are already running and the connected Android devices.

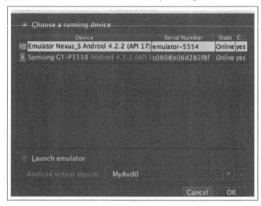

If you do not want to use any of the running devices, click on "Launch emulator" in the lower half of the window and select a suitable device from the "Drop-Down menu".

The "Run" window displays messages related to progress.

Finally, the app will run on the selected emulator or Android device.

Running the app from the command line

The fact that Android Studio works with the Gradle Build System enables several options to work at the command line level.

Proceed as follows to create an unsigned debug and release APK of the MyApplication app project:

Use the cd option in the terminal window to go to the MyApplication project directory.

For Windows:

```
gradlew.bat assemble
```

For Linux and Mac:

```
./gralew assemble
```

You will then see the two files under:

/MyApplication/ MyApplication/build/apk:

      MyApplication-debug-unaligned.apk

      MyApplication-release-unsigned.apk

The option to working with Gradle build scripts is often used when working with remote test servers. See the links for the Build Server examples.

The significance of AndroidManifest.xml and build.gradle

The AndroidManifest.xml and build.gradle files are configuration files that must be included in every app. The Android Manifest.xml file

The AndroidManifest.xml file contains metadata of the app that is required for the Android system and for operating the project. It is the central description data of an app.

In the Hello World! example, there is only one activity; it is automatically the first one that is called. However, there are more than one activity in case of large app projects. Which would be the first one called after opening the app?

It is normally the activity that was created using the "New Project" wizard when creating a new project. If you have created the project on your own, you obviously know the name of this first activity. However, if you have received the code from someone else, you can view the AndroidManifest.xml file to find out the activity having the Start status.

Android Manifest is an XML document that contains essential components of an Android application. This document contains:

The Java package name

Components of the application:

- ➡ Icon name
- ➡ Activities with their attributes
- ➡ Services
- ➡ Broadcast receiver
- ➡ Content provider
- ➡ Permissions (authorisations)
- ➡ Minimum API-Level is now a part of build.gradle

The activity listed first is called when the app is started.

```xml
<activity
    android:name="com.greendog.androidstudio.example.dinoquiz.QuizActivity"
    android:label="DinoQuiz" >
    <intent-filter>
        <action android:name="android.intent.action.MAIN" />

        <category android:name="android.intent.category.LAUNCHER" />
    </intent-filter>
</activity>
```

Both entries, namely *android.intent.action.MAIN* and *android.intent.category.LAUNCHER* are responsible for creating an icon for this activity on the screen (Launcher). Normally, only one icon is required to start an app. It is however possible to place an icon for each activity on the screen. An example is given later.

What can you do with this Hello World app? The app is a good starting point on which you can build your own apps. The structure is already in place. If you want to convert the app into your own app idea, you need to modify the layout file containing text such that it corresponds to your intended design. If required, you can create more files until the app idea is implemented. We will do exactly this in the following app projects.

THE BUILD.GRADLE FILE

The new Gradle Build System was simultaneously introduced along with the new development environment. The build.gradle file contains all information that is required for building an app, i.e. to create one or more APKs from the raw project files.

The important fact is that, when building an app, the Minimum Android Version is no longer read from the AndroidManifest.xml file, but from the build.gradle file.

All libraries that need to be used by the app must be included in the build.gradle file.

The Gradle chapter in the annexe gives more detailed information about Gradle.

Overview of IDE

Similar to most other programmes, Android Studio has a menu bar and a toolbar. I will not go through all menus, but point out only those menu items and icons that I think are important for beginners.

The following figure shows the empty workspace of Android Studio with toolbars on the sides and on top.

1. The menu bar and the toolbar
If it is not showing, enable the toolbar in the View menu.
2. The buttons for opening different views
3. The empty work space is filled with the views depending on the buttons that you click.

A few tips for navigation and file management are displayed at the centre of the work space that is still empty.

The <Alt>+<1> shortcut key for opening the project view and the <Ctrl>+<E> shortcut key for displaying the last edited files are really practical. A complete list is given in the Help menu.

The topmost line of the work space shows the project name, the storage location and the current Android Studio version.

Menu bar

The "File" menu contains all configuration settings which you can also access from the Welcome screen.

"Close Project": it closes the currently opened project and returns to the Welcome screen.

"Exit" or Android Studio -> Quit Android Studio: it closes the project as well as Android Studio.

The "Build" menu contains the sub-menu to sign an app. More information about signing an app is given in the "Preparing the app for the Android market" chapter.

In addition to the commands relevant for "Run", the "Run" menu item also has settings for the "Run" configuration under "Edit Configuration". For example, whether an emulator should be started automatically or whether the selection window for selecting an emulator is displayed before starting an app.

The "Tools" menu item primarily has sub-menus such AVD Manager or SDK Manager that are relevant for Android.

You can also access these Android-specific menus from the toolbar.

You can add "Version Control Integration" to the project under the VCS menu. More information about VCS is given in the annexe.

The last menu item is "Help", which contains tables for shortcut keys among other things.

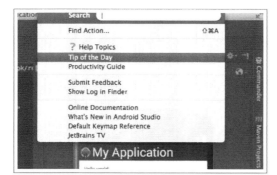

The row under the toolbar shows the path of the opened director and the opened file.

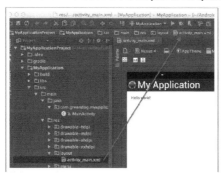

Configuring the editor

From the menu file → Other Settings → Default Settings

select "Code Style" to adapt the editor.

Tips and tricks for the editor

If you are working in a layout file in the Text mode, a live preview of the layout is shown to the right of the editor window.

For displaying line numbers, go to

View → Active Editor → Show Line Numbers

In order to detected "hard coded strings" in Java files, which should ideally be in a strings.xml file, go to Analyse → Inspect Code.

After the search process, the result will be displayed in Android Lint → Hard coded text.

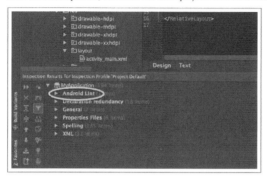

Renaming

You can rename variables or constants in a Java file by bringing the mouse pointer to this constant or variable and using the shortcut key <Shift><F6>. One of the special features of the intelligent editor is shown here. All dependencies that are associated with this variable/constant are automatically updated after renaming.

Generating strings on the fly

The editor allows generating or changing "strings"/ character sequences "on the fly".

Example to change a text: The text in our app should be changed from "HelloWorld" to "Hello Android World".

In the opened *"activity-main.xml"* file, bring the mouse pointer to

```
android:text="@string/hello_world"
```

and change "hello_world" to "android_world"

```
"@string/android_word"
```

@string is now marked in red to indicate that content for this variable cannot be found.

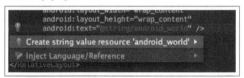

This is because there is no content for the variable.

It can be created by pressing the key combination <Alt> <Enter>

From the pop-up menu, select

Create string and enter 'android_world' as the name of the resource.

Once you select this, a dialogue window will be shown. Here you can enter the desired content "Hello Android World" in the "Resource value" field and confirm with <OK>.

The colour of variable name changes from red to green and you can see the new text in the live preview.

If you simply want to change the text of an existing variable, click on the variable name using the mouse and then enter the following key combination:

<Apple key> <B> for Mac

<Windows key> <B> for Windows

<CTRL><B> for Linux

to navigate to the file that you want to change.

Example: changing the font size

At the moment, the font size is not specified in the TextView of the layout file; this means that Android uses a default size.

We want to increase the font size and use the "dimens.xml" file for this purpose. A dimens.xml file is created by default when creating a project. However, it does not contain any entry for the "Hello Android World" text.

First add the following to the TextView of the *activity_main.xml* file

```
android:textSize="@dimen/androi_world_size"
```

Then use the shortcut key

<Alt><Enter> to invoke the pop-up menu and click on

"Create dimen value resource 'androi_world_size'"

Enter the desired size, e.g. 32 dp, and confirm with <OK>.

The live preview shows the new size directly.

More tips for the editor are shown in "Tips of the Day".

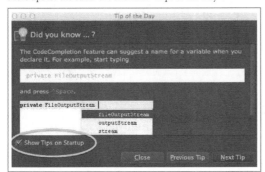

If you have deselected the checkbox to display the "Tip of the Day" automatically, you can view these tips from the Help menu.

APP LAYOUT DESIGN: TEXT / DESIGN EDITOR

Android Studio has an advanced layout editor that you can use to add Drag-and-Drop-Widgets in the layout and can preview the layout while editing the XML file.

A live preview is generated while editing in the text view. The preview window has different options for the device settings, layout theme, platform version, etc. In order to simultaneously show the layout on multiple devices, go to the "Preview" drop-down icon in the left corner and select -> Preview All Screen Sizes.

While editing a layout file, you can always toggle between the Design mode and the Text mode.

Example: Creating the Android app project: MySwipeImageViewer

In the Design mode, you can add components to the layout using the Drag and Drop method. In this example, an image was added after modifying the default text.

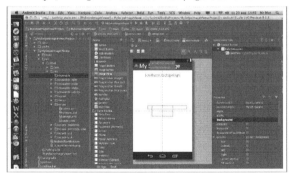

You can select the resources that you have earlier copied in the relevant folder.

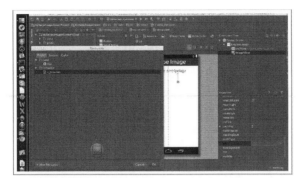

You can always toggle between the Text and Design modes. If you are in the Text mode, a live preview of the layout is automatically shown.

Resources such as text for buttons or dimensions can be created 'on the fly' as described above.

Creating a folder for another language

In the project window, right-click on

the res/ folder -> New -> Android resource directory

If you want to see how the layout looks on different screen sizes, you can do it directly from the editor by clicking the icon in the top-left corner in the Preview window and selecting the Display Layout option.

In this case, we have selected: Preview Representative Sample

Second project: DinoQuiz trivia game

This project is intended to make you aware about the concepts of Android development.

In addition, the app is provided with layout elements that are used in nearly every app. These are text elements (text widget), graphic elements (image widget) and buttons (button widget).

The finished app has multiple screens (views). The first screen is display after starting the app; it shows a selection menu; once you select the Play option, the first question will be displayed. You can then use "Next" and "Back" buttons to navigate to next and previous questions respectively.

THE APP IDEA

The app, which we will create, is DinoQuiz. It will test users' knowledge about dinosaurs through questions. A question is asked and different options are provided to select an answer. The game displays a feedback message depending on whether the answer was correct or wrong. There are 5 questions in all.

We will now create this game in multiple steps.

Creating the layout for the first screen

Our objective is to create the following screen:

First close the Hello World app via File -> Close Project

Now create a new project for DinoQuiz using the New Project option.

You can create the app icon as per your liking. Tip: Use Google Images to search for a suitable image and change it to a square shape before including it in the project. Although the PNG format is the preferred image format for Android, JPG also functions perfectly.

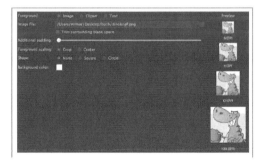

The name of the start activity for the quiz should be **QuizActivity** (to follow the example project). Adopt the file name for the layout file as recommended by Android Studio.

Otherwise, you can proceed as in case of the Hello World project, adopt the default values and click on Next and Finish.

After Android Studio builds a project, it normally presents it in the form of an opened layout file.

The editor is in the Text mode and a live preview of the layout is shown to the right of the editor.

In the first step, we will remain in the Text mode and change the Relative layout to the Linear layout.

Android has series of predefined layouts (view groups):

The **Linear layout** allows a linear positioning of child elements, i.e. vertical or horizontal

The **Relative layout** allows relative positioning of elements with respect to each other

The **Table layout** represents child elements in rows and columns

In the **Grid view**, a list adapter automatically adds the child elements to a two-dimensional scrollable grid

The **Tab layout** view group comprises three elements. The TabHost is the root node in the hierarchy, the Tabwidget contains the contents of the view in a frame layout. You can use the TabHost to toggle between different views of activities in this layout depending on the implementation

The **List view** displays child elements in a scrollable list

The **Frame layout** is used for organising the widgets, especially when they overlap.

The Linear layout is best-suited for our app project.

The Android user interface comprises two base elements:

Views: Base elements of the interface. The View class is the base of the so-called "widgets" which represent the fully implemented UI elements

View groups: A view group is a container for different views and serves as a base class for the "layouts" that enable positioning of views.

You can tile the view groups as per your requirement and build a hierarchy tree. While outlining the interface, each view group requires its child nodes starting from the root node and downwards in order to ensure its complete representation. Although views can define a size and a position, the final appearance of an element strongly depends on the parameters of the associated parent node, i.e. the layout.

First change the TextView:

You must change the text and the position on the screen.

For this, go the Design mode of the editor by clicking on the <Design> button.

Then double-click on the "Hello World" text to open the context menu and to create a new variable for our text.

Enter for example the following as a new string value resource:

Resource name: question_text

Resource value: Are birds nearest relatives of dinosaurs?

In order to place the text in the Linear layout such that is centre-aligned vertically and horizontally, click on the Lineal layout in the "Component tree" and change the values for "gravity" and "orientation" in "Properties".

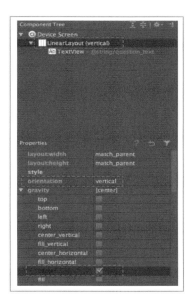

Our next task is to add two buttons.

The current Linear layout is vertically aligned. If you directly add both buttons here, one button would be placed on top of the other, and not next to each other as desired in our app idea.

You need to define a new Linear layout (horizontal) below the text to be able to place these buttons next to each other. You can then "Drag and Drop" the buttons.

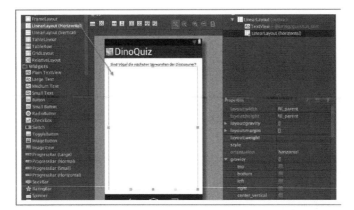

The Linear layout (horizontal) was added via "Drag and Drop".

In this layout, you need to drag the widget button 2 times and place them next to each other. The Lineal layout around the buttons will then be reduced to the size of buttons. The Properties option is used for this.

layout width is set

from fill_parent (entire width) to

wrap_content (only as wide as required)

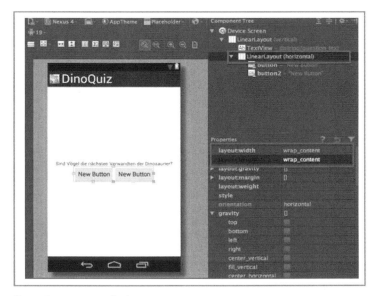

Repeat the same process for the entry

`layout height`

In the next step, we will define the names of buttons and increase the distance from the text.

Adapting the buttons

Double-click on the left button and create a new string resource as described in the "Changing the Hello World text" section. Repeat the same process for the right button.

For the left button, enter the following as a new string value resource:

Resource name: true_button

Resource value: correct

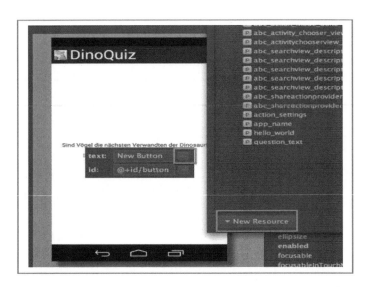

For the right button, enter the following as a new string value resource:

Resource name: false_button

Resource value: wrong

You can increase the distance between the buttons and the text by setting a value for *layout margin* in Properties.

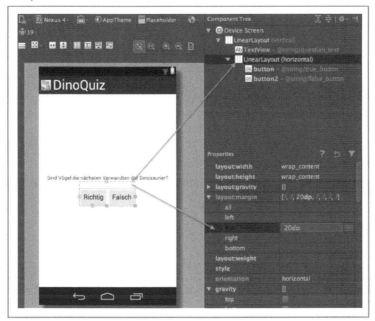

dp

Density-independent-pixel is a relative variable specification that is always used when the app is supposed to run on different screen sizes with different resolutions. The dp unit is based on a screen resolution of 160 dpi. This means that 1 dp = 1 px (pixel) on a device with 160 dpi.

On a screen with 240 dpi, 1 dp is = 1.5 px. The conversion formula is: $px = dp * (dpi / 160)$.

The first screen now looks as we have planned. When you now click on the <Text> button to return to the text mode of the editor, you can see the code that was created for widgets.

While we have built new string value resources, they were stored in values/strings.xml.

```xml
<?xml version="1.0" encoding="utf-8"?>
<resources>

    <string name="app_name">DinoQuiz</string>
    <string name="hello_world">Hello world!</string>
    <string name="action_settings">Settings</string>
    <string name="question_text">Sind Vögel die nächsten Verwandten der Dinosaurier?</string>
    <string name="true_button">Richtig</string>
    <string name="false_button">Falsch</string>

</resources>
```

Instead of the Design mode, you can carry out all these activities in the Text mode and write the code manually.

ASSIGNING FUNCTIONS TO BUTTONS

Both buttons, namely Correct and Wrong, should respond on clicking and display suitable text on the screen depending on whether the answer was correct or wrong. This means that we must establish a contact between the button definition in the layout file and the activity (QuizActivity.java) which can respond to the user actions and executes one of the actions predefined by us.

Life cycle

The life cycle of the app desired by us presently looks as follows: Starting the app

-> QuizActivity -> activity_quiz.xml

-> A button is clicked -> QuizActivity -> Display message

How can QuizActivity respond to the button click? Resources such as images and text are stored in a R.java file. An activity retrieves information about a resource from this R.java file using the ID. In figure 2.13, you can see that the Correct button has the button ID:

```
<Button
android:layout_width="wrap_content"
android:layout_height="wrap_content"
android:text="@string/true_button"
android:id="@+id/button" />
```

If you want to access a resource from an activity, you must first allocate an ID to it. From the activity, the "Correct button" resource accessed as shown below:

```
findViewByID(R.id.button)
```

You can allocate the ID as per your choice and need not accept the default values button and button2. In most cases, it is advisable to select names that indicate the function of buttons. We will rename both IDs to true_button and false_button; the definition of button will then be:

```
<Button
android:layout_width="wrap_content"
android:layout_height="wrap_content"
android:text="@string/true_button"
android:id="@+id/true_button" />

<Button
android:layout_width="wrap_content"
android:layout_height="wrap_content"
android:text="@string/true_button"
android:id="@+id/false_button" />
```

Also change the access definition for buttons accordingly: findViewByID(R.id.true_button) or findViewByID(R.id.false_button)

Edit the QuizActivity.java activity as well

The QuizActivity.java activity is already open. We will go to the QuizActivity.java tab.

Until now, the QuizActivty contains only the code that was automatically generated when creating the project. `package com.greendog.androidstudio.example.dinoquiz;`

```
import android.app.Activity;
import android.os.Bundle;
import android.view.Menu;

public class QuizActivity extends Activity {

@Override
protected void onCreate(Bundle savedInstanceState) {
super.onCreate(savedInstanceState);
setContentView(R.layout.activity_quiz);
}
@Override
public boolean onCreateOptionsMenu(Menu menu) {
// Inflate the menu; this adds items to the action bar if it is present.
getMenuInflater().inflate(R.menu.quiz, menu);
return true;
}
}
```

ACTIVITIES

An activity is the elementary component of an application that offers an interaction option to the user. You can create or import an interface in an activity using setContentView; the interface normally occupies the entire screen or is embedded in another activity. Various events might occur in the life cycle of an activity and change the activity status, e.g. a tap on the Home button or an incoming call can push an activity in the foreground to the background. The activity life cycle considers these influences in the application. When a class inherits from an activity, it can overwrite the onCreate(), onStart(), onResume(), onPause(), onStop(), onDestroy() and onRestart() method so that it can appropriately respond to a change in the status. The call of onStop() is separately listed here since the user need not forcefully execute this directly; onStop() can be executed when another activity comes in the foreground again through onResume() and conceals this. This is also possible due to a newly started activity.

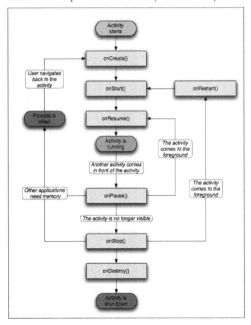

The preceding image shows different phases of an activity and possible subsequent statuses. The life cycle of an activity starts from the first call of onCreate() and ends with the call of onDestroy() which releases all utilised resources of the activity. The visible life cycle ranges from the call of onStart() to the call of onStop(); these methods can be called several times in the runtime of the activity depending on the frequency with which it is pushed in the foreground or the background. During this time, the user can see this activity in the foreground although interactions are not possible sometimes in this period. An interaction is possible only between the calls of onResume() and onPause().

The QuizActivity.java activity has oı.ly 2 methods:

onCreate(Bundle savedInstanceState)

onCreateOptionsMenu(Menu menu)

The first one is required to create a separate sub-class of the activity. In our example, it is QuizActivity. The second method creates the menu that can be seen in the Action Bar whenever desired. (Hello World example). It only has a place-holder function at the moment.

At present, we are using only a fraction of the life cycle offered by Android. This will change as we make progress with our programming.

Intents are required to switch from one activity to the other. An intent is an abstract object that is used for starting an activity, notifying a broadcast receiver or for communicating with a service. We will need an intent later when we click the new "Next" button that leads to another screen.

However, we will first connect the existing buttons with QuizActivity so that it triggers an action.

In order to disclose the buttons for QuizActivity, we need to create two "member variables", i.e. one each for every button. The following is added to QuizActivity:

```
...
public class QuizActivity extends Activity {
private Button mTrueButton;
private Button mFalseButton;
@Override
protected void onCreate(Bundle savedInstanceState) {
super.onCreate(savedInstanceState);
setContentView(R.layout.activity_quiz);
}
...
```

The Text button is red and thus indicates an error. When you hover the mouse pointer over the Word button, the following message is shown: cannot resolve symbol 'Button'.

When you double-click on the button, a key combination to resolve the problem is displayed. This key combination differs depending on the operating system. The following figure shows the key combination for Mac.

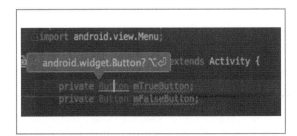

You can use the key combination <ALT> <ENTER> to open a context menu that is used for adding the missing import.

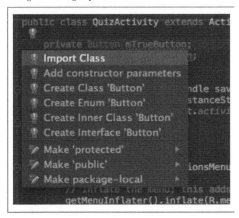

Confirm the import with <Enter>. The android.widget.Button; import will then be added to the list of imports. You can also add imports manually; however, you might not what is exactly required in each case.

We will first establish a connection with the resources of buttons:

```
@Override
protected void onCreate(Bundle savedInstanceState) {
super.onCreate(savedInstanceState);
setContentView(R.layout.activity_quiz);
mTrueButton = (Button)findViewById(R.id.true_button);
mFalseButton = (Button)findViewById(R.id.false_button);
}
```

A so-called "Listener" is required to ensure that the buttons respond to a click. The corresponding listener is called "onClickListener". Add the following for the Correct button (mTrueButton):

```
@Override
protected void onCreate(Bundle savedInstanceState) {
super.onCreate(savedInstanceState);
setContentView(R.layout.activity_quiz);

mTrueButton = (Button)findViewById(R.id.true_button);
mTrueButton.setOnClickListener(new View.OnClickListener() {

@Override
public void onClick(View v) {
// will be added later
}
 });

mFalseButton = (Button)findViewById(R.id.false_button);
}
```

Add the following for the Wrong button (mFalseButton):

```
@Override
protected void onCreate(Bundle savedInstanceState) {
super.onCreate(savedInstanceState);
setContentView(R.layout.activity_quiz);
mTrueButton = (Button)findViewById(R.id.true_button);
mTrueButton.setOnClickListener(new View.OnClickListener() {

@Override
public void onClick(View v) {
// will be added later
}
});
mFalseButton = (Button)findViewById(R.id.false_button);
mFalseButton.setOnClickListener(new View.OnClickListener() {

@Override
public void onClick(View v) {
// will be added later
}
});
 }
```

Both buttons are now waiting for a click; however, we have not yet defined as to what should happen after a click. A place-holder in the form of the following comment is currently used here

// will be added later

When editing the code, keep in mind that the editor has an "autofill" function and always offers a series of recommendations. This saves a lot of typing work and prevents spelling mistakes.

In the next step, we will ensure that the click on button is responded with a message. The Text in our example project provides 2 language resources (values, values-en). If your system language on the device or Emulator is Geman, you will see the text similar to the screenshot. Is your system language English, you will see the text for the Buttons and for the Toast in English. You can easy add your own language by adding a new values directory with a strings.xml in your language.

We requires a class called "Toast" for this type of feedback. The toast requires a string resource (R.string.correct_toast) and must know the length of the message display (Toast.LENGTH_LONG). SHORT and LONG length options are available. The string resource can be created in the same manner as the one described for buttons.

Add the following to QuizActivity:

```
mTrueButton = (Button)findViewById(R.id.true_button);
mTrueButton.setOnClickListener(new View.OnClickListener() {

@Override
public void onClick(View v) {
Toast.makeText(QuizActivity.this,
R.string.correct_toast,
                Toast.LENGTH_LONG).show();
        }
    });
```

For the correct answer of the question, enter the following as a new string value resource:

Resource name: correct_toast

Resource value: This is correct!

```
mFalseButton = (Button)findViewById(R.id.false_button);
mFalseButton.setOnClickListener(new View.OnClickListener() {
@Override
public void onClick(View v) {
Toast.makeText(QuizActivity.this,
R.string.incorrect_toast,
Toast.LENGTH_LONG).show();
                }
        });
 }
```

For the wrong answer of the question, enter the following as a new string value resource:

Resource name: incorrect_toast

Resource value: Unfortunately, this is wrong!

More questions, one new class and one new button will be added

Questions should be displayed in succession. You can use the "Next" button to go to another question.

We will now add nine questions and the text for the "Next" button in the *strings.xml* file.

```
<?xml version="1.0" encoding="utf-8"?>
<resources>
<string name="app_name">DinoQuiz</string>
<string name="hello_world">Hello world!</string>
<string name="action_settings">Settings</string>
<string name="question_birds">Are birds nearest relatives of dinosaurs?</
string>
<string name="question_nessi">The Nessi sea monster is the last surviving
dinosaur</string>
<string name="question_jurassic">The Jurassic Park is a nature reserve for
dinosaurs</string>
<string name="question_veggi">All dinosaurs were vegetarian</string>
<string name="question_biggest">Rex was the biggest dinosaur</string>
<string name="true_button">Correct</string>
<string name="false_button">Wrong</string>
<string name="next_button">Next</string>
<string name="correct_toast">This is correct!</string>
<string name="incorrect_toast">Unfortunately, this is wrong!</string>
</resources>
```

We will first edit the *activity_quiz.xml* file.

We need to add an ID to the TextView since we want to access this location from QuizActivity as a resource. The text to be displayed when the app starts is stored in the new who_knows variable (strings.xml). Enter the following as a new string value resource for who_knows:

Resource name: who_knows

Resource value: Who knows the answer?

Once a user clicks on "Next", QuizActivity determines the text to be displayed in the *question_text_view* TextView.

```
<TextView
android:id="@+id/question_text_view"
android:text="@string/who_knows"
android:layout_width="wrap_content"
android:layout_height="wrap_content" />
```

We will now add the new "Next" button:

```
<Button
android:layout_width="wrap_content"
android:layout_height="wrap_content"
android:text="@string/false_button"
android:id="@+id/false_button" />
</LinearLayout>
<Button
android:layout_width="wrap_content"
android:layout_height="wrap_content"
android:text="@string/next_button"
android:id="@+id/next_button" />    </LinearLayout>
```

A NEW CLASS WILL BE CREATED

For this, right-click on the folder of the class. In this example, allocate
com.greendog.androidstudio.example.dinoquiz under java/.

New -> Java Class and specify TrueFalse as its name. The structure should then look as follows:

Add the following to TrueFalse.java:

```
public class TrueFalse {
private int mQuestion;
// This variable stores the resource ID for a string, resource ID is always
int
private boolean mTrueQuestion;// This variable indicates whether a question
is true or false
public TrueFalse(int question, boolean trueQuestion) {
     mQuestion = question;
          mTrueQuestion = trueQuestion;
     }
```

Both the variables, namely mQuestion and mTrueQuestion, require so-called getter and setter
access methods to be able to retrieve or modify individual properties of an object. You can thus
modify the implementation without changing its public interface. Getter == retrieval method
Setter == modification method

The *getter* and *setter* methods are automatically added in Android Studio. You simply need to
configure the prefixes to be used for "member variables" in Android Studio to enable this
automated mechanism.

Disclosing the prefixes in Android Studio

File -> Other Settings -> Default Settings -> Code Style -> Java -> Code Generation In this case, **m** is used a prefix for the field and **s** is used as prefix for the static field

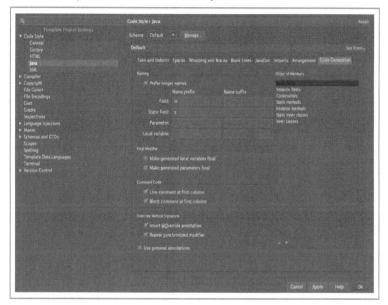

You can then add the getter and setter methods of TrueFalse.java by selecting the TrueFalse constructor, invoking the *Generate* context menu using **CTRL + ENTER** and selecting *Getter and Setter*.

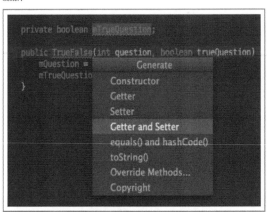

Select both variables and confirm with <OK>. "It's like Magic!"

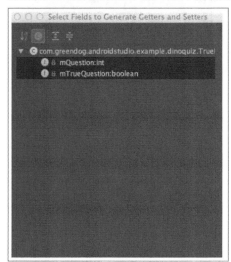

The generated code should look as follows:

```
public class TrueFalse {

private int mQuestion;
private boolean mTrueQuestion;
public int getQuestion() {

return mQuestion;
}

public void setQuestion(int question) {
mQuestion = question;
}

public boolean isTrueQuestion() {

return mTrueQuestion;
}
public void setTrueQuestion(boolean trueQuestion) {
mTrueQuestion = trueQuestion;
}

public TrueFalse(int question, boolean trueQuestion) {
mQuestion = question;
mTrueQuestion = trueQuestion;
}
}
```

TrueFalse.java is now complete. It can be used by QuizActivity.

Our Model-View-Controller model (MVC) currently has the following components:

In this construction, TrueFalse assumes the task of the "model" and QuizActivity assumes the role of the "controller". "Views" are defined by "widgets" in the activity_quiz.xml file.

Modifications in QuizActivity

We need 2 new variables - one of the "Next" button and the other for the TextView in the activity_quiz.xml file to be able to establish communication between both objects. Both new variables will be added ...

Button mFalseButton;

Button mNextButton;

TextView mQuestionTextView;

The "Next" button will be added as mNextButton:

...

```
mFalseButton = (Button)findViewById(R.id.false_button);
mFalseButton.setOnClickListener(new View.OnClickListener() {
@Override
public void onClick(View v) {
checkAnswer(false);
}
});
mNextButton = (Button)findViewById(R.id.next_button);
mNextButton.setOnClickListener(new View.OnClickListener() {
@Override
public void onClick(View v) {
mCurrentIndex = (mCurrentIndex + 1) % mAnswerKey.length;
updateQuestion();
}
});
```

The array for accessing the questions:

```
TrueFalse[] mAnswerKey = new TrueFalse[] {
new TrueFalse(R.string.question_birds, true),
new TrueFalse(R.string.question_jurassic, false),
new TrueFalse(R.string.question_nessi, false),
new TrueFalse(R.string.question_veggi, false),
new TrueFalse(R.string.question_biggest, false)
};
```

The questions to the displayed in TextView must be updated.

```
int mCurrentIndex=0;
private void updateQuestion() {
int question = mAnswerKey[mCurrentIndex].getQuestion();
mQuestionTextView.setText(question);
}
```

To ensure that the correct Toast is displayed, it must be checked whether the question has been defined as correct or wrong.

```
private void checkAnswer(boolean userPressedTrue) {
boolean answerIsTrue = mAnswerKey[mCurrentIndex].isTrueQuestion();
      int messageResId;
      if (userPressedTrue == answerIsTrue) {
messageResId = R.string.correct_toast;
} else {
messageResId = R.string.incorrect_toast;
}
Toast.makeText(this, messageResId, Toast.LENGTH_LONG)
.show();
}
```

The test in the emulator or on the device shows the following when we start the app:

.. and the following when we click on <Next>

Display in the portrait mode

Display in the landscape mode

A different layout should be used for the landscape mode to ensure that the button is not concealed by the Toast. More information regarding layouts is given in the Layout section.

When you see the construction of the mNextButton for Next, it is not difficult to guess how a Back button would look.

We will now add a "Previous" button and pep-up the layout slightly

We will first add the "Previous" button in the *activity_quiz.xml* layout file.

Since we want to place two button next to each other, these will be embedded in a **horizontal Linear layout** similar to Correct and Wrong.

```
<LinearLayout
android:orientation="horizontal"
android:layout_width="wrap_content"
android:layout_height="wrap_content"
android:baselineAligned="false"
android:paddingTop="60dp">


<Button
android:layout_width="wrap_content"
android:layout_height="wrap_content"
android:text="@string/prev_button"
android:id="@+id/prev_button"
android:paddingLeft="10dp"
android:paddingRight="20dp"
android:layout_marginRight="30dp" />
 <Button
android:layout_width="wrap_content"
android:layout_height="wrap_content"
android:text="@string/next_button"
android:id="@+id/next_button"
android:paddingLeft="10dp"
android:paddingRight="20dp"
android:layout_marginLeft="30dp" />
</LinearLayout>
```

"Previous" is assigned as resource value for prev_button.

Adding the button in the activity

We will add a variable for the Previous button in QuizActivity:

Button mPrevButton;

Add the function of mPrevButton in QuizActivity

```
mPrevButton = (Button)findViewById(R.id.prev_button);
mPrevButton.setOnClickListener(new View.OnClickListener() {
@Override
public void onClick(View v) {
mCurrentIndex = (mCurrentIndex - 1) % mAnswerKey.length;
                updateQuestion();
}
});
```

Increasing the text size and centring it

```
<TextView
android:id="@+id/question_text_view"
android:layout_width="wrap_content"
android:layout_height="wrap_content"
android:text="@string/who_knows"
android:textAppearance="?android:attr/textAppearanceLarge"
android:layout_gravity="center_horizontal"
android:gravity="center_horizontal" />
```

Instead of "textAppearance", you can also use textSize to change the font size.

Example:

```
android:textSize="24sp"
```

We recommend using "sp" as the unit of measurement for letters since it supports scaling. Other layout improvements include changing the shape and colour of buttons or adding a coloured background.

Example of background colours:

In 'Component Tree', you can select individual layout elements and assign separate background colours to them.

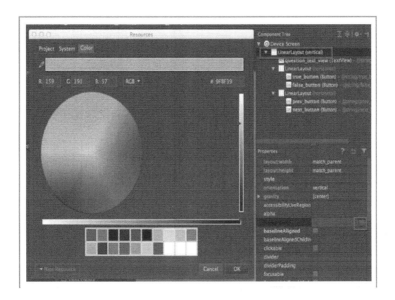

Example for the final App

Android offers only one type of text buttons by default. For example, if you want buttons with rounded edges, you need to define "Shape Drawables". A Shape Drawable is an XML file that is stored in the drawable/ folder.

Shape Drawable

In the following example, we will create a Shape Drawable for the "Next" and "Previous" navigation buttons.

First create the drawable/ folder at the same level as that of the existing drawable-hdpi, etc. Then create a new XML file named *nav_buttons.xml* in this folder and add the following contents:

```xml
<?xml version="1.0" encoding="utf-8" ?>
<selector xmlns:android="http://schemas.android.com/apk/res/android">

<item android:state_pressed="true" >
<shape>
<gradient
android:startColor="#ff43ff48"
android:endColor="#ff264f18"
android:angle="270" />
<stroke
android:width="1dp"
android:color="#ff708628" />
<corners
android:radius="6dp" />
<padding
android:left="10dp"
android:top="10dp"
android:right="10dp"
android:bottom="10dp" />
</shape>
</item>

<item>
<shape>
<gradient
android:startColor="#ff38abef"
android:endColor="#ff233c6c"
android:angle="270" />
<stroke
android:width="1dp"
android:color="#ff237c92" />
<corners
android:radius="6dp" />
<padding
android:left="10dp"
android:top="10dp"
android:right="10dp"
android:bottom="10dp" />
</shape>
</item>
</selector>
```

In activiy_quiz, replace the background colour with the Shape Drawable

`android:background="@drawable/nav_buttons"`

You can repeat the same procedure for the "Correct" and "Wrong" buttons by creating a new XML file named true_false.xml in this folder. You can assign different colours to the button and give it a three dimensional look.

A possible end result and the end of the second project is shown below.

The third project: Android Easter Eggs

The core focus of the third project is on layouts. It should be possible to present the given contents with different layouts.

The following elements are available for contents:

- Text: Android version
- Text: API version
- Text: Code name of Android version
- Image: Logo of Android version
- Image: Easter Egg of Android version

A problem that you often encounter is described below; you want to display a list of elements from which the user selects one element and the new content is displayed when the users clicks on this element. One of the options is to provide a clickable selection list using a ListView. The ListView can comprises text or text and images. Another option is the GridView that is especially suitable when the selection list to be displayed comprises images.

Both these popular layouts have been used for the following examples of presenting the selection lists/menus:

ListView

GridView

LISTVIEW

The end result should consist of a ListView that has a detailed view for every element in the list, e.g.:

When creating the new project, you can allocate the same names used in the last project to both layout files since a fragment layout is not required even this time.

3 layout files are required for showing the list displayed above. The first defines that we want use ListView to display a list containing the desired number of elements that are positioned one below the other. The ListView is also responsible to ensure that the contents can be scrolled if the list contains more elements than that supported by the screen.

The first layout file named *activity_main.xml* is shown here.

The second layout file defines the layout of individual elements. Its name is *list_item_layout.xml*.

The third layout file is required to display the Easter Egg. Its name is *detail.xml*.

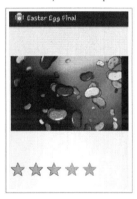

Adding resources to the project

Image resources are required for this project; mini-images for the ListView and Easter Egg images for the second screen.

For images, we will first create a separate folder named

drawable/

Right-click on the res/ folder -> New -> Directory and assign the "drawable" name to the folder.

A drawable folder is to be used when you do not want provide different images for different screen resolutions such as drawable-hdpi, drawable-mdpi, etc. For every application, it must be individually decided whether different large images are required.

When you add images to a project, ensure that the memory reservation for the image(s) does not become excessively large.

Example: The Easter Egg image for Android KitKat

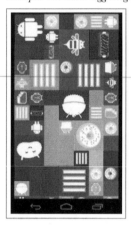

The original image size is 236 KB if you see it in Explorer on a computer. Its resolution is 1080 x 1920 pixel. The file size of 236 KB is not too large. However, how much space will the image need when it is loaded in Android? Android requires 4 KB per pixel. The calculation is as follows:

4 x 1080 x 1920 = 8,294,400 KB

1 MB = 1024 KB

8 294 400 ./. 1024 = 8.1 MB

Android thus requires 8.1 MB to load the image.

At present, only 16 MB of the RAM can be used for a running app. Depending on the size of the remaining app, this image size may crash the app.

The situation can be improved by reducing the resolution and using JPG formats; this can be done outside Android Studio using image editing software such as Gimp, Photoshop, etc. After reducing the image resolution to 227 × 403 pixel, it requires only 357 KB in Android.

➡ Time required to download images and copy them to drawable/.

Creating the ListViews layout

Rename the activity_main.xml file to main.xml. For this, right-click on the file -> Refactor -> Rename.

Then add the following contents to the main.xml file:

```
<LinearLayout
android:orientation="vertical"
android:layout_width="fill_parent"
android:layout_height="fill_parent"
xmlns:android="http://schemas.android.com/apk/res/android">


<ListView
android:layout_width="wrap_content"
android:layout_height="wrap_content"
android:id="@+id/quotes_list"
android:layout_gravity="center_horizontal"/>
</LinearLayout>
```

The ListView is here encapsulated by a LinearLayout. Theoretically, you can do away with the LinearLayout. The advantage of this structure is that you can add more elements to the LinearLayout such as a space for ads or a search bar. Additional elements other than the ListView elements cannot be added to the ListView.

The ListView is called by the *ReaderActivity.java* activity using:

```
@Override
    public void onCreate(Bundle savedInstanceState) {
            super.onCreate(savedInstanceState);
            setContentView(R.layout.main);
```

Add elements to the ListView

Each element should comprise an image and a text.

We will need a new file for this purpose. Right-click on the Layout folder and select

-> New -> Layout resource file

and name the *list_item_layout.xml* file. Replace the contents of the opened file with the following:

```xml
<?xml version="1.0" encoding="utf-8"?>
<RelativeLayout xmlns:android="http://schemas.android.com/apk/res/android"
android:layout_width="match_parent"
android:layout_height="match_parent"
android:paddingLeft="@dimen/activity_horizontal_margin"
android:paddingRight="@dimen/activity_horizontal_margin"
android:paddingTop="@dimen/activity_vertical_margin"
android:paddingBottom="@dimen/activity_vertical_margin">

<ImageView
android:id="@+id/thumb"
android:layout_width="60dp"
android:layout_height="60dp"
android:layout_centerVertical="true"
android:layout_alignParentLeft="true"/>

<TextView
android:id="@+id/text"
android:layout_toRightOf="@+id/thumb"
android:layout_width="wrap_content"
android:layout_height="wrap_content"
android:textSize="18sp"
android:layout_marginLeft="10dp"
android:layout_centerVertical="true"
android:singleLine="false"
android:ellipsize="end"
android:textStyle="bold" />
</RelativeLayout>
```

We have selected a RelativeLayout for the definition of list elements so that the image and the text can be placed next to each other. The ImageView contains the image, the TextView contains the text that is displayed next to the image.

Both widgets get IDs so that they can be later accessible from the Java file. Since the text for some elements is longer than the line, android:singleLine="false" was set here.

If you want to use only one line irrespective of the length of the text, you can use the following options

android:singleLine="true"

android:ellipsize="end"

to truncate the end of the line and replace it with dots.

If the contents of a screen are dynamically generated, you will need an adapter (Java file) that retrieves data from the "data source" in the layout. This adapter can be generated using ArrayAdapter, CursorAdapter or BaseAdapter.

Adapters are required for the ListView as well as for the GridView.

We will first create a data source that can then be accessed by the adapter.

Creating the data source

We must first provide resources by copying all required images in the drawable/ folder(s) (here only drawable/) and adding the resources string (texts) in the strings.xml file.

After downloading the GitHub project, we can copy images from the drawable/ folder to our project.

We will need to add the following string resources to the *strings.xml* file:

```
<string name="quote_1">Android 1.5 Cupcake API 3</string>
<string name="quote_2">Android 1.6 Donut API 4</string>
<string name="quote_3">Android 2.0.x-2.1 Eclair API 5-7</string>
<string name="quote_4">Android 2.2.x Froyo API 8</string>
<string name="quote_5">Android 2.3.x Gingerbread API 9,10</string>
<string name="quote_6">Android 3.x.x Honeycomb API 11-13</string>
<string name="quote_7">Android 4.0.x Ice Cream Sandwich API 14,15</string>
<string name="quote_8">Android 4.1.x-4.3.x Jelly Bean API 16-18</string>
<string name="quote_9">Android 4.4 KitKat API 19</string>
<string name="quote_10">Android 5 Candy Apple API XX</string>
```

Create a new Java file, name it *DataSource* and add the following source code:

```java
import java.util.ArrayList;
public class DataSource {
private ArrayList<Integer> mPhotoPool;
private ArrayList<Integer> mQuotePool;
private ArrayList<Integer> mPhotoHdPool;

        public ArrayList<Integer> getmPhotoHdPool() {
            return mPhotoHdPool;
        }

        public ArrayList<Integer> getmPhotoPool() {
            return mPhotoPool;
        }

        public ArrayList<Integer> getmQuotePool() {
            return mQuotePool;
        }

    private void setupPhotoPool() {
        mPhotoPool.add(R.drawable.donut);
        mPhotoPool.add(R.drawable.cupcake);
        mPhotoPool.add(R.drawable.eclair);
        mPhotoPool.add(R.drawable.froyo);
        mPhotoPool.add(R.drawable.gingerbread);
        mPhotoPool.add(R.drawable.honeycomb);
        mPhotoPool.add(R.drawable.icecreamsandwich);
        mPhotoPool.add(R.drawable.jellybean);
        mPhotoPool.add(R.drawable.kitkat);
        mPhotoPool.add(R.drawable.candyapple);
    }
        private void setupQuotePool() {
        mQuotePool.add(R.string.quote_1);
        mQuotePool.add(R.string.quote_2);
        mQuotePool.add(R.string.quote_3);
        mQuotePool.add(R.string.quote_4);
        mQuotePool.add(R.string.quote_5);
        mQuotePool.add(R.string.quote_6);
        mQuotePool.add(R.string.quote_7);
        mQuotePool.add(R.string.quote_8);
        mQuotePool.add(R.string.quote_9);
        mQuotePool.add(R.string.quote_10);
    }
        private void setupPhotoHDPool() {
        mPhotoHdPool.add(R.drawable.donut_ee);
        mPhotoHdPool.add(R.drawable.cupcake_ee);
        mPhotoHdPool.add(R.drawable.eclair_ee);
        mPhotoHdPool.add(R.drawable.froyo_ee);
        mPhotoHdPool.add(R.drawable.gingerbread_ee);
        mPhotoHdPool.add(R.drawable.honeycomb_ee);
        mPhotoHdPool.add(R.drawable.icecreamsandwich_ee);
        mPhotoHdPool.add(R.drawable.jellybean_ee);
        mPhotoHdPool.add(R.drawable.kitkat_ee);
        mPhotoHdPool.add(R.drawable.candyapple_ee);
    }
```

Function for storing the length of the array list

```
    public int getDataSourceLength() {
        return mPhotoPool.size();
    }
// Constructor
    public DataSource() {
        mPhotoPool = new ArrayList();
        mQuotePool = new ArrayList();
        mPhotoHdPool = new ArrayList();
        setupPhotoPool();
        setupQuotePool();
        setupPhotoHDPool();
    }
}
```

3 variables have been created for the logo image in the ListView (mPhotoPool), for the text in the ListView and the detail view (mQuotePool) and for the image in the detail view (mPhotoHdPool).

Getter methods were generated for variables.

Individual arrays will be filled with data

Finally, variables in the constructor were initialised.

Creating the adapter

The adapter will be added to the *ReaderActivity.java* activity. The following code will be added to the class:

```
 public class ReaderActivity extends Activity {
     public class QuoteAdapter extends BaseAdapter {
         private Context mContext;
private LayoutInflater mInflator;
private DataSource mDataSource;
         public QuoteAdapter(Context c) {
mContext = c;
mInflator = (LayoutInflater)
mContext.getSystemService(Context.LAYOUT_INFLATER_SERVICE);
mDataSource = new DataSource();
}

@Override
public int getCount() {
return mDataSource.getDataSourceLength();
}
@Override
public Object getItem(int position) {
return position;
}
```

```
@Override
public long getItemId(int position) {
return position;
}

@Override
public View getView(int position, View convertView, ViewGroup parent) {
ImageView thumbnail;
TextView quote;
if(convertView == null) {
convertView = mInflator.inflate(R.layout.list_item_layout, parent, false);
}

thumbnail = (ImageView) convertView.findViewById(R.id.thumb);
thumbnail.setImageResource(mDataSource.getmPhotoPool().get(position));
quote = (TextView) convertView.findViewById(R.id.text);
quote.setText(mDataSource.getmQuotePool().get(position));
return convertView;
}
}
```

A new variable called *mInflator* was added.

It is used to instantiate the layout XML files in the corresponding view objects.

getCount(): returns the number of elements in the data set

getItem(int position): retrieves the data for the corresponding position of the element

getItemId(int position): retrieves the line ID of the element

getView(int position, View convertView, ViewGroup parent): retrieves the data for the view to be displayed

The getView function is the main function. It is responsible for binding the data from the data source with the list view element.

After creating the data source and the adapter, we must specify in the *ReaderActivity.java* activity that it should use the adapter:

Establishing a connection between the adapter and ReaderActivity

We will add the following code to the ReaderActivity.java file:

Add the following to the variables:

```
private ListView mListView;
```

Add the following to the onCreate method:

```
@Override
    public void onCreate(Bundle savedInstanceState) {
        super.onCreate(savedInstanceState);
        setContentView(R.layout.main);
        mListView = (ListView) findViewById(R.id.quotes_list);
        mListView.setAdapter(new QuoteAdapter(this));
```

Creating a new screen

After clicking an element from the list, the so-called "Easter Egg" of the corresponding Android version should be displayed. We will first create a layout file that repeats the Easter Egg image and the text from the list.

Creating the second screen

Like before, right-click on the layout/ folder to create a new XML file called *detail.xml* with the following contents:

```xml
<?xml version="1.0" encoding="utf-8"?>
    <RelativeLayout
        xmlns:android="http://schemas.android.com/apk/res/android"
        android:layout_width="fill_parent"
        android:layout_height="fill_parent"
        android:paddingLeft="@dimen/activity_horizontal_margin"
        android:paddingRight="@dimen/activity_horizontal_margin">
        <ImageView
            android:id="@+id/image"
            android:layout_alignParentTop="true"
            android:layout_width="fill_parent"
            android:layout_height="350dip"
            android:src="@drawable/donut" />
        <TextView
            android:id="@+id/quote"
            android:layout_width="fill_parent"
            android:layout_height="wrap_content"
            android:layout_below="@+id/image"
            android:textSize="18sp"
            />
    </RelativeLayout>
```

A series of configuration options are available for RelativeLayout, ImageView and TextView. These can be best viewed when the editor is in the Design mode. You sometime know the often used configurations by heart, but these cannot be guessed. Android is sometimes called "moving target". The moment you think it is in your sight, it moves (further development).

You will need an activity to display the detail.xml layout file on the screen: Create the activity for the second screen

Create a new Java file called Detail. The Detail.java file should have the following code:

```
...
public class Detail extends Activity {
private ImageView mImageView;
private TextView mQuote;
private int mPosition;
private DataSource mDataSource;
@Override
protected void onCreate(Bundle savedInstanceState) {
super.onCreate(savedInstanceState);
setContentView(R.layout.quote_detail);
Intent i = getIntent();
mPosition = i.getIntExtra("position", 0);
mDataSource = new DataSource();
mImageView = (ImageView) findViewById(R.id.image);
mQuote = (TextView) findViewById(R.id.quote);
mImageView.setImageResource(mDataSource.getmPhotoHdPool().get(mPosition));
mQuote.setText(getResources().getString(mDataSource.getmQuotePool().get(mPosi
tion)));
}
}
```

Connecting both screens with each other

In most cases, you can go to the next screen by clicking a button or a selection element. In our case, a clock on an elements in the ListView should trigger an action. We will first need an observer who registers when which elements from the list was clicked. Add the following to the ReaderActivity activity that is responsible for displaying the ListView:

```
...
mListView = (ListView) findViewById(R.id.quotes_list);
mListView.setAdapter(new QuoteAdapter(this));
mListView.setOnItemClickListener(new AdapterView.OnItemClickListener() {
```

An intent must be created to switch to a new screen.

A new intent is built using the following code whenever an element from the list is clicked. The position of the element is sent with putExtra. The position can be processed in the Detail activity for which the query is sent; it also provides the image and the text for the position.

```java
@Override
public void onItemClick(AdapterView<?> arg0, View arg1, int position,
long arg3) {
Intent i = new Intent(ReaderActivity.this, Detail.class);
i.putExtra("position", position);
startActivity(i);
        }
});
    }
}
```

Each activity of an app must have an entry in the AndroidManifest.xml configuration file. Both these entries should be included in the AndroidManifest.xml file.

```xml
<activity
android:name=".ReaderActivity"
android:label="@string/app_name">
<intent-filter>
<action android:name="android.intent.action.MAIN" />
<category android:name="android.intent.category.LAUNCHER" />
</intent-filter>
</activity>
<activity android:name=".Detail"
android:screenOrientation="portrait">
</activity>
```

GRIDVIEW

The GridView shows the selectable elements in a 2 dimensional grid; individual elements of the grid have the same size and the automatically aligned. Since this layout is primarily used for image elements, the example should represent the problem solution.

Similar to the ListView example, the GridView requires an image adapter to access images.

The simple form of the GridView has a set of mini images that are shown in the grid. When you click on one of these images, it will be displayed in a new view with full resolution.

The end result will be as shown in the following figure:

Two layout files that represent two different screens are required for the project. The first screen contains the GridLayout with logos of Android versions and the second one shows the corresponding Easter Egg for the selected Android version.

Since the same images as those used in the ListView example should be used for this project, these must be added to the project again. Therefore, first create the drawable/ folder and then copy images to it.

Several Java classes must be created as well. Also needed are Adapter containing information for images, the Activity for displaying the GridView screen and the Activity for displaying the Detail screen of the selected element.

Creating layouts for the GridView

The file: *grid_layout.xml*

```xml
<?xml version="1.0" encoding="utf-8"?>
<GridView xmlns:android="http://schemas.android.com/apk/res/android"
android:layout_marginTop="@dimen/activity_vertical_margin"
android:layout_marginBottom="@dimen/activity_vertical_margin"
android:layout_marginLeft="@dimen/activity_horizontal_margin"
android:layout_marginRight="@dimen/activity_horizontal_margin"
android:id="@+id/grid_view"
android:layout_width="fill_parent"
android:layout_height="fill_parent"
android:numColumns="auto_fit"
android:columnWidth="120dp"
android:horizontalSpacing="10dp"
android:verticalSpacing="10dp"
android:gravity="center"
android:stretchMode="columnWidth" >
</GridView>
```

The 4 layout_margin lines ensure adequate distance from the edge of the screen.

columnWidth defines the width of the grid frame for an element/image. The image width and image size is not specified here, but set in the *AndroidGridLayoutActivity.java* file that will be created later.

Spacing lines are used to provide distance between the grid elements.

stretchMode columnWith ensures that the entire width of the screen is used and additional intermediate space is provided if required.

The file: *full_image.xml*

```xml
<?xml version="1.0" encoding="utf-8"?>
<LinearLayout xmlns:android="http://schemas.android.com/apk/res/android"
android:layout_width="match_parent"
android:layout_height="match_parent"
android:orientation="vertical" >

<ImageView android:id="@+id/full_image_view"
android:layout_width="fill_parent"
android:layout_height="fill_parent"/>
</LinearLayout>
```

Create an image adapter

Create a new Java file called *ImageAdapter.java*.

```
package com.greendog.androidstudio.example.eastereggggridview;
import android.content.Context;
import android.view.View;
import android.view.ViewGroup;
import android.widget.BaseAdapter;
import android.widget.GridView;
import android.widget.ImageView;
public class ImageAdapter extends BaseAdapter {private Context mContext;
// Images Array for GridView
public Integer[] mThumbIds = {
R.drawable.cupcake, R.drawable.donut,
R.drawable.eclair, R.drawable.froyo,
R.drawable.gingerbread, R.drawable.honeycomb,
R.drawable.icecreamsandwich, R.drawable.jellybean,
R.drawable.kitkat, R.drawable.keylimepie
    };
// Constructor
public ImageAdapter(Context c){mContext = c;}
    @Override
public int getCount() {return mThumbIds.length;}
    @Override
public Object getItem(int position) {return mThumbIds[position];}
    @Override
public long getItemId(int position) {return 0;}
    @Override
public View getView(int position, View convertView, ViewGroup parent) {
ImageView imageView = new ImageView(mContext);
imageView.setImageResource(mThumbIds[position]);
imageView.setScaleType(ImageView.ScaleType.CENTER_CROP);
imageView.setLayoutParams(new GridView.LayoutParams(100, 100));
return imageView;}}
```

This image adapter is typical for a standard GridView.

The image adapter creates an array called mThumbIds. This means that we will, at the moment, provide only the images for the GridView with the logos for Android versions. When a user clicks one of these images, the second screen shows this image in its full size. However, the plan was to show another picture, namely the image of the Easter Egg for the corresponding Android version, on the second screen. An additional array is required for the second image. We will create it in the next step.

```
imageView.setLayoutParams(new GridView.LayoutParams(100, 100));
```

defines the image size. It must be less than the grid that is specified in the *grid_layout.xml* file.

Creating an activity for the GridView

File: AndroidGridLayoutActivity.java

```
package com.greendog.androidstudio.example.eastereggggridview;
import android.app.Activity;
import android.content.Intent;
import android.os.Bundle;
import android.view.View;
import android.widget.AdapterView;
import android.widget.AdapterView.OnItemClickListener;
import android.widget.GridView;
public class AndroidGridLayoutActivity extends Activity {

@Override
public void onCreate(Bundle savedInstanceState) {
super.onCreate(savedInstanceState); setContentView(R.layout.grid_layout);
GridView gridView = (GridView) findViewById(R.id.grid_view);
// Instance of ImageAdapter

Class gridView.setAdapter(new ImageAdapter(this));
 /** * On Click event for Single GridView Item * */

gridView.setOnItemClickListener(new OnItemClickListener() {

@Override
public void onItemClick(AdapterView<?> parent, View v, int position, long id)
{
// Sending image id to FullScreenActivity
Intent i = new Intent(getApplicationContext(), FullImageActivity.class);
// passing array index
i.putExtra("id", position); startActivity(i);
}
});
}
}
```

The task of the *AndroidGridLayoutActivity.java* file is to build the GridView along with the grid_layout.xml layout file. Individual images in the GridView are associated with an OnItemClickListener that records a click on the image and forwards the information about the position of the image to the next FullImagActivity.java activity, which is used to display the image in its full size.

File: *FullImageActivity.java*

```
package com.greendog.androidstudio.example.eastereggridview;

import android.app.Activity;
import android.content.Intent;
import android.os.Bundle;
import android.widget.ImageView;

public class FullImageActivity extends Activity {
@Override
public void onCreate(Bundle savedInstanceState) {
super.onCreate(savedInstanceState); setContentView(R.layout.full_image);

// get intent data
Intent i = getIntent();

// Selected image id
int position = i.getExtras().getInt("id");

ImageAdapter imageAdapter = new ImageAdapter(this);
ImageView imageView = (ImageView) findViewById(R.id.full_image_view);
imageView.setImageResource(imageAdapter.mThumbIds[position]);
}
 }
```

The line

```
imageView.setImageResource(imageAdapter.mThumbIds[position]);
```

is responsible to determine the image to the displayed. To be precise, it select the array pool from which the image originates. If another image needs to be displayed in the second screen, you must specify the array that contains the image. Adding another array

In the *ImageAdapter.java* file, the new array for the second image is directly set below the first array; this new array contains the names of mFullImageIds.

```
// Images Array for GridView
public Integer[] mThumbIds = {
R.drawable.cupcake, R.drawable.donut, R.drawable.eclair, R.drawable.froyo,
R.drawable.gingerbread, R.drawable.honeycomb, R.drawable.icecreamsandwich,
R.drawable.jellybean, R.drawable.kitkat, R.drawable.keylimepie
};
```

```
// Images Array for FullImageActivity
public Integer[ ] mFullImageIds = {
R.drawable.cupcake_ee, R.drawable.donut_ee,
R.drawable.eclair_ee, R.drawable.froyo_ee,
R.drawable.gingerbread_ee, R.drawable.honeycomb_ee,
R.drawable.icecreamsandwich_ee, R.drawable.jellybean_ee,
R.drawable.kitkat_ee, R.drawable.keylimepie_ee
        };
```

Then modify the following line in the *FullImageActivity.java* file: change

imageView.setImageResource(imageAdapter.mThumbIds[position]);

to

imageView.setImageResource(imageAdapter.mFullImageIds[position]);

so that the new image is retrieved from the correct array.

GRIDLAYOUT

The difference between GridView and GridLayout

In the GridView, all elements have the same size and are stored in a 2-dimensional grid. The GridView has a scrollbar. It contains its elements from the ListAdapter.

In the GridLayout, the size of each element can be defined individually.

For detailed documentation, please refer to:

http://developer.android.com/reference/android/widget/GridLayout.html

Application example for the GridLayout: Layout for a pocket calculator

In the following example, we will not create a functional pocket calculator, but only its layout. An example of calculation in an Android app is given in the BMI calculator chapter.

The layout file for the pocket calculator

```
<?xml version="1.0" encoding="utf-8"?>
<GridLayout xmlns:android="http://schemas.android.com/apk/res/android"
android:layout_width="wrap_content"
android:layout_height="wrap_content"
android:layout_gravity="center"
android:columnCount="4"
android:orientation="horizontal" >
<Button
android:layout_column="3"
android:text="/" />
<Button android:text="1" />      <Button android:text="2" />      <Button
android:text="3" />      <Button android:text="*" />      <Button
android:text="4" />      <Button android:text="5" />      <Button
android:text="6" />      <Button android:text="-" />      <Button
android:text="7" />      <Button android:text="8" />      <Button
android:text="9" />
<Button
android:layout_gravity="fill"
android:layout_rowSpan="3"
android:text="+" />
<Button
android:layout_columnSpan="2"
android:layout_gravity="fill"
android:text="0" />
<Button android:text="00" />
<Button
android:layout_columnSpan="3"
android:layout_gravity="fill"
android:text="=" />  </GridLayout>
```

Explanation of the code:

The number of columns is defined by android:columnCount="4".

One of the specialities of the GridLayout is that columns can remain unused as shown in the first line of the layout:

```
android:layout_column="3"
android:text="/" />
```

Unused cells can be filled vertically and horizontally:

Vertical: The Plus (+) sign

```
android:layout_gravity="fill"
android:layout_rowSpan="3"
android:text="+" />
```

Horizontal: The equals (=) sign

```
android:layout_columnSpan="3"
android:layout_gravity="fill"
android:text="=" />
```

An interesting application example for creating a form using the GridLayout is given on the Google's Android blog:

http://android-developers.blogspot.se/2011/11/new-layout-widgets-space-and-gridlayout.html

The fourth project: BMI calculator

This chapter contains:

- TableLayout
- LinearLayout
- ImageView
- TextView
- Spinners
- Weights
- Calculation operations

When one conceptualise an app, one normally starts with a sketch on paper and then refines the appearance using image editing software such as Photoshop, Gimp or Inkscape. One then searches for the Android design pattern (LinearLayout, TableLayout) and widgets (TextView, ImageView, Spinner, Button) that are best suited for the desired appearance. Often, multiple solutions are available to create a layout. This also applies to the following app. The example shows a possible solution. The following structure has been selected for this app:

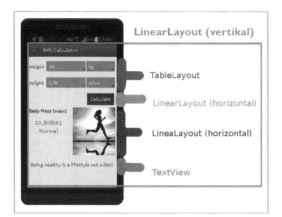

Roughly said, the layout has 4 blocks that are embedded in a LinearLayout. Individual blocks contain embedded layout and widgets.

We will first create a new project. We required a single layout. We need to include special support libraries and we can give any desired name to the app. The layout for the app

Open the *activity_main.xml* layout file and delete its contents.

We will first add the LinearLayout (vertical).

```
<?xml version="1.0" encoding="utf-8"?>
<LinearLayout xmlns:android="http://schemas.android.com/apk/res/android"
android:layout_width="fill_parent"
android:layout_height="fill_parent"
android:orientation="vertical">
</LinearLayout>
```

We will now gradually add blocks from top to bottom.

Adding the TableLayout

The TableLayout has 2 TableRow widgets. Each TableRow contains 1 TextView and 2 spinners. The TableLayout is set under the line android:orientation="vertical">:

```xml
<TableLayout
android:id="@+id/tableLayout1"
android:layout_width="match_parent"
android:layout_height="wrap_content" >

<TableRow
android:id="@+id/tableRow1"
android:layout_width="wrap_content"
android:layout_height="wrap_content"
android:layout_marginLeft="5dp"
android:layout_marginRight="5dp"
android:layout_marginTop="15dp" >

<TextView
android:id="@+id/textView1"
android:layout_width="wrap_content"
android:layout_height="wrap_content"
android:layout_marginRight="5dp"
android:text="@string/weightLabel"
android:textAppearance="?android:attr/textAppearanceMedium"
android:textColor="@color/black" />
<Spinner
android:id="@+id/spinner1"
android:layout_width="fill_parent"
android:layout_height="wrap_content"
android:prompt="@string/weightLabel"
android:layout_weight="2" />


<Spinner
android:id="@+id/spinner2"
android:layout_width="fill_parent"
android:layout_height="wrap_content"
android:layout_weight="1"
android:entries="@array/weightUnitsArray" />
</TableRow>


<TableRow
android:id="@+id/tableRow2"
android:layout_width="wrap_content"
android:layout_height="wrap_content"
android:layout_marginLeft="5dp"
android:layout_marginRight="5dp"
```

```
    android:layout_marginTop="15dp" >

    <TextView
    android:id="@+id/textView2"
    android:layout_width="wrap_content"
    android:layout_height="wrap_content"
    android:layout_marginRight="5dip"
    android:text="@string/heightLabel"
    android:textAppearance="?android:attr/textAppearanceMedium"
    android:textColor="@color/black" />

    <Spinner
    android:id="@+id/spinner3"
    android:layout_width="fill_parent"
    android:layout_height="wrap_content"
    android:prompt="@string/heightLabel"
    android:layout_weight="2" />

    <Spinner
    android:id="@+id/spinner4"
    android:layout_width="fill_parent"
    android:layout_height="wrap_content"
    android:layout_weight="1"
    android:entries="@array/heightUnitsArray" />
    </TableRow>
    </TableLayout>
```

SETTING UP A SO-CALLED SPINNER

The above code contains spinners at different locations. Spinners are selection menus. The elements to be provided in the selection menu can be defined in a TAG array in the strings.xml file.

```
<!-- Strings arrays used in Spinner widgets -->
<string-array name="heightUnitsArray">
<item >feet/inch</item>
<item >m/cm</item>
</string-array>
<string-array name="weightUnitsArray">
<item >lb</item>
<item >kg</item>
</string-array>
```

Elements can be accessed from the Java file using the array names.

One more LinearLayout containing a button widget is embedded in the LinearLayout. It is placed below the end of the TableLayout. In this part of the layout, you can define the alignment of individual widgets. Unlike the outer LinearLayout, this is aligned horizontally.

```
<LinearLayout
android:layout_width="wrap_content"
android:layout_height="wrap_content"
android:layout_gravity="center_horizontal"
android:orientation="horizontal"
android:layout_marginTop="15dp">

<Button
android:id="@+id/button1"
android:layout_width="match_parent"
android:layout_height="wrap_content"
android:layout_marginBottom="10dp"
android:layout_marginRight="0dp"
android:onClick="calculateClickHandler"
android:text="@string/calculateButton"
android:layout_gravity="center_horizontal"
android:layout_alignParentStart="true"/>
</LinearLayout>
```

Additional elements of the layout can be added depending on the app structure shown at the beginning.

The layout file has multiple connection points for

The *BMICalculatorActivity* Java file:

the array names "heightUnitsArray" and "weightUnitsArray" for menus

the "button1" button for calculation

and "textView4" and "textView5" TextViews for the result

```
<TextView
android:id="@+id/textView4"
android:layout_width="match_parent"
android:layout_height="wrap_content"
android:gravity="center_horizontal"
android:text=""
android:textAppearance="?android:attr/textAppearanceLarge" />

<TextView
android:id="@+id/textView5"
android:layout_width="match_parent"
android:layout_height="wrap_content"
android:gravity="center_horizontal"
android:text=""
android:textAppearance="?android:attr/textAppearanceLarge" />
```

The activity contains comments for individual areas and tasks:

https://github.com/janebabra/Android_lernen_am_Beispiel/blob/master/
MyBMIApplication/bmiapp/src/main/java/com/greendog/example/bmiapp/
BMICalculatorActivity.java

The fifth project: True or False

Core focus of this chapter:

- ScrollView

- Layout for the portrait and landscape formats

When you need a ScrollView, you can use specific layouts that automatically have a scrolling function. For example, these layouts are ListView and GridView. Other layouts like LinearLayout and RelativeLayout do not have a built-in scrolling function. As shown in the example, if an app has a RelativeLayout, a scrolling function must be added using a ScrollView if the contents are longer than one screen.

The application example can be downloaded from GitHub.

In the screenshot, you can clearly see that the layout contains multiple elements, TextViews and ImageViews. However, a ScrollView may contain only ONE element. Therefore, all elements are first placed in a RelativeLayout. We then enclose the RelativeLayout with a ScrollView.

The screen displayed above is the *activity_main.xml* layout file in the layout/ folder.

Creating layouts for the portrait and landscape formats

If you want to vary the display of contents in the landscape format and the portrait format, create a separate layout file named *activity_main.xml* for the landscape format and store it in the **layout-land/ folder**.

This option is often used to display the same contents with different layouts. You can also use different screen definitions to display the questions in a game in the portrait format and answers in the landscape format.

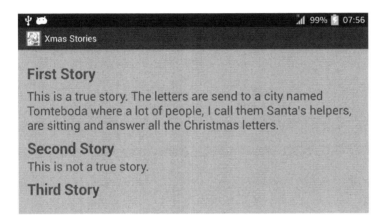

The sixth project: WebView & Co.

This chapter focuses on different ways to integrate website contents in an Android app or called in an app.

Other topics in this chapter are:

• MediaPlayer

• Life cycle

• Logging

• Activities and launcher

The app comprises 3 activities that integrate the website contents in the app using different methods. There is a 4th activity that displays HTML contents and is attached to the MyApplication project (the First project chapter) as an info file.

INTERNAL ANDROID BROWSER

The first activity of the app: Der Hund der Baskervilles (The Hound of the Baskervilles)

The app is supposed to do the following: It compiles the text of the summary of The Hound of the Baskervilles along with an image from the story and also has a button called Wiki with which the web page of the wiki of the Hound of the Baskervilles can be launched. The internal Android browser is used for calling the web page. A background music is played while the text with the image is displayed. If a user exits the activity by clicking a button and switches to the web page, the music should stop. If the user returns to the story (using a Back button), the music should be restarted. The music is played using Android MediaPlayer. This MediaPlayer has a series of control options. The MediaPlayer can be used to study the lifecycle of an app in detail.

After creating a new project using a single layout, create a new folder called raw/ in the res/ folder. You can copy the mp3 file that needs to be played as background music in this folder.

Copy the image (dog.png) for the story in drawable-mdpi.

Remove the Hello World text from the layout.

In the graphics mode of the layout editor:

Drag an ImageView in the empty layout and select src, drawable/ dog under Properties.

Place a plain TextView widget below the image.

We will need a String variable (baskevilles_text) to add the planned text.

Add the following in the strings.xml file:

```
<string name="baskevilles_text">
Sherlock Holmes — The Hound of the Baskervilles
Summary of the story
Dr. Mortimer lowered his voice and nearly whispered while telling detective
Sherlock Holmes and his friend and assistant Dr. John Watson about the sudden
and mysterious death.... The text is shortened here.
</string>
```

Now you can use the following variable in the TextView in the *activity_main.xml* layout file:
android:text="@string/baskevilles_text"

The result should look like the following:

"Sherlock Holmes — The Hound of the Baskervilles"
Summary

 The Hound of the Baskervilles opens with a mini
mystery—Sherlock Holmes and Dr. Watson
speculate on the identity of the owner of a cane that
has been left in their office by an unknown visitor.
Wowing Watson with his fabulous powers of
observation, Holmes predicts the appearance of
James Mortimer, owner of the found object and a
convenient entrée into the baffling curse of the
Baskervilles. Entering the office and unveiling an
18th century manuscript, Mortimer recounts the
myth of the lecherous Hugo Baskerville. Hugo
captured and imprisoned a young country lass at
his estate in Devonshire, only to fall victim to a
marauding hound of hell as he pursued her along
the lonesome moors late one night. Ever since,
Mortimer reports, the Baskerville line has been
plagued by a mysterious and supernatural black
hound. The recent death of Sir Charles Baskerville
has rekindled suspicions and fears. The next of kin.

Quotation marks, such as those in the first line, are provided with a backslash so that Android identifies them as part of the text.

In order to keep the space of one line between the heading and the text, we can use formatting options such as preceding backslash; these are also known as "escape sequences".

Java/Android supports the following escape sequences:

line feed, horizontal tab, form feed, carriage return, single quote, double quote, backslash

In the screenshot, you can see that the entire text is not fitted on the screen. If you want to run the app in the emulator or on a telephone, you can sometimes see only a part of the text.

The extent of displayed text depends on the resolution. We will add a ScrollView to our layout to ensure that the entire text can be read on the device.

```
<ScrollView xmlns:android="http://schemas.android.com/apk/res/android"
xmlns:tools="http://schemas.android.com/tools"
android:layout_width="match_parent"
android:layout_height="match_parent">
<RelativeLayout xmlns:android="http://schemas.android.com/apk/res/android"
xmlns:tools="http://schemas.android.com/tools"
android:layout_width="match_parent"
android:layout_height="match_parent"
android:paddingLeft="@dimen/activity_horizontal_margin"
android:paddingRight="@dimen/activity_horizontal_margin"
android:paddingTop="@dimen/activity_vertical_margin"
android:paddingBottom="@dimen/activity_vertical_margin">
<ImageView
android:layout_width="wrap_content"
android:layout_height="wrap_content"
android:id="@+id/imageView"
android:layout_alignParentTop="true"
android:layout_centerHorizontal="true"
android:src="@drawable/dog"/>
<TextView
android:layout_width="wrap_content"
android:layout_height="wrap_content"
android:text="@string/baskervilles_text"
android:id="@+id/textView"
android:layout_below="@+id/imageView"
android:layout_centerHorizontal="true"
android:layout_marginTop="33dp"/>
</RelativeLayout>
</ScrollView>
```

As the last step for the layout, we will add a button for the link of the wiki page using a **LinearLayout:**

```
<TextView
android:layout_width="wrap_content"
android:layout_height="wrap_content"
android:text="@string/baskervilles_text"
android:id="@+id/textView"
android:layout_below="@+id/imageView"
android:layout_centerHorizontal="true"
android:layout_marginTop="33dp"/>
<LinearLayout
android:layout_below="@+id/textView"
android:orientation="horizontal"
android:layout_width="match_parent"
android:layout_height="match_parent"
android:gravity="center_horizontal|bottom">


<Button
android:id="@+id/button"
android:layout_width="wrap_content"
android:layout_height="wrap_content"
android:text="Wiki"
android:layout_alignParentBottom="true"
android:onClick="openWiki"/>
</LinearLayout>
</RelativeLayout> </ScrollView>
```

The layout now has the desired appearance.

ADDING THE MEDIA PLAYER

In the next step, we will edit the MainActivity.java file to add the MediaPlayer for the background music and to link the wiki button with the wiki page.

We must first import the class to be able to use the MediaPlayer in the activity:

```
import android.media.MediaPlayer;
```

For the MediaPlayer, we will create a variable called *backgroundmusic* that can be used to call and influence the MediaPlayer in the further course.

```
public class MainActivity extends ActionBarActivity {
MediaPlayer backgroundmusic;
@Override
protected void onCreate(Bundle savedInstanceState) {
super.onCreate(savedInstanceState);
setContentView(R.layout.activity_main);
```

We will now add the code to start the MediaPlayer.

The mp3 file backgroundmusic.mp3 is imported by resources (R.raw.backgroundmusic).

```
public class MainActivity extends ActionBarActivity {
MediaPlayer backgroundmusic;
@Override
protected void onCreate(Bundle savedInstanceState) {
super.onCreate(savedInstanceState);
setContentView(R.layout.activity_main);
backgroundmusic = MediaPlayer.create(this, R.raw.backgroundmusic);
backgroundmusic.start();
}
```

After adding the MediaPlayer, we will add the following to the code in order to open the "Wiki" button at the end of the text.

```
// open button: Wiki - in the layout
android:onClick="openWiki is included
public void openWiki(View v) {
String url = "http://de.wikipedia.org/wiki/Der_Hund_von_Baskerville";
Intent intent = new Intent(Intent.ACTION_VIEW);
intent.setData(Uri.parse(url));
startActivity(intent);
}
```

LIFE CYCLE

We will add onPause and onResume to handle different situations of the lifecycle. Methods of the lifecycle, e.g. onCreate, onPause, onResume, onStop, onDestroy, are also known as callbacks.

```
@Override
protected void onPause() {
backgroundmusic.stop();
backgroundmusic.release();
super.onPause();
}

@Override
protected void onResume() {
backgroundmusic.start();
super.onResume();
}
```

onPause

It responds to interruptions. This is the case when the activity is exited while the Wiki button is clicked and the wiki page is loaded in the foreground or when a call is received.

onResume

It responds when a user returns to the activity after an interruption.

Logcat offers excellent verification options for the life cycle and the sequence through various "callbacks". This can be used to detect errors that were not observed so easily or not observed at all during the practical testing of the app.

When we start the app, the following things happen:

The Baskerville activity starts. It loads the text on the screen and plays the background music. After clicking the Wiki button, the wiki page is opened in the Android browser; this means that the Baskerville activity is exited. However, it is still active in the background, but is not visible. If a user clicks the Back button, the Baskerville activity again returns to the foreground and we can see the text again. Howe, the music does not play. This is a bug. In order to see what happens after clicking the Back button, we will use the log system (Logcat) of Android.

LOGCAT (SYSTEM LOG)

The Logcat of Android smartphones is a so-called system logger that is always active in the Android operating system. Each app and every process that is active on the smartphone have the option of writing different types of messages in this log. Normally, the messages to be read are too technical and are not relevant for normal users and do not enhance the functioning of an app. They are usually helpful only to the developers of apps to be able to analyse the errors arising during operation in a better manner. Log information can be added in the app code at desired places to display the status information in the log window. The LogCat is the central repository of all messages related to the system and apps. Error messages and other information can be stored in it and read using an IDE or directly on the device using suitable apps.

When developing your own apps, you can log messages or errors caught in the LogCat. This is possible using five different types; all these types are based on the same syntax.

The syntax is as follows:

Log.X(tag, message);

You must replace X with the suitable message type:

v -> "verbose" (unimportant and can be ignored in most cases)

i -> information (rather unimportant and is often ignored)

d -> debug (information only for the development)

w -> warning (important information; however, the error does not hamper the remaining app)

e -> error (important information; should never occur)

The LogCat also requires the specification of a TAG. This can be freely selected, but should be the same throughout your app. In my example, this TAG is "Fehlersuche" (error search). It is a common convention to select the activity name as a TAG. This makes sense when you have an app, wherein multiple activities are connected with each other. A "message" should be selected such that it corresponds to the position of the Logcat, i.e. describes the task that should be executed at this position.

You will need the following Import definition to be use the Logcat in the app:

```
import android.util.Log;
@Override
protected void onCreate(Bundle savedInstanceState) {
Log.e("Fehlersuche", "onCreate");
super.onCreate(savedInstanceState);
setContentView(R.layout.activity_main);
backgroundmusic = MediaPlayer.create(this, R.raw.backgroundmusic);
backgroundmusic.start();
}
```

```
@Override
protected void onResume() {
backgroundmusic.start();
Log.e("Fehlersuche", "onResume");
super.onResume();
}

@Override
protected void onPause() {
backgroundmusic.stop();
backgroundmusic.release();
Log.e("Fehlersuche", "onPause");
super.onPause();
}
```

If you now run the app (on telephone or emulator), you can see the log entries from our code and errors, if any, in the Logcat window at the bottom.

The error in the Logcat shows that the error has occurred in conjunction with onResume, i.e. when we return to the activity. Android Studio often displays error messages in the plain text format; however, only an error code can be seen here:

start called in state 64 error (-38,0)

When you search for this error code (Google), you will realise that the MediaPlayer cannot be called after onPause or onStop. In onResume, the MediaPlayer should be directly started with backgroundmusic.start();. The MediaPlayer however requires a prepared status before it can be started. Such information is given in the state diagram of the MediaPlayer.

http://developer.android.com/reference/android/media/MediaPlayer.html You can achieve the "Prepared Status" with the call

```
backgroundmusic = MediaPlayer.create(this, R.raw.backgroundmusic);
```

that is currently in the onCreate method.

In order to resolve the problem in onResume, you can remove the prepared state and the start of the MediaPlayer from onCreate and add it to onResume.

```
backgroundmusic = MediaPlayer.create(this, R.raw.backgroundmusic);
backgroundmusic.start();
```
The code should now look as follows:

```
@Override
protected void onCreate(Bundle savedInstanceState) {
Log.e("Fehlersuche", "onCreate");
super.onCreate(savedInstanceState);
setContentView(R.layout.activity_main);
}

@Override
protected void onResume() {
backgroundmusic = MediaPlayer.create(this, R.raw.backgroundmusic);
backgroundmusic.start();
Log.e("Fehlersuche", "onResume");
super.onResume();
}

@Override
protected void onPause() {
backgroundmusic.stop();
backgroundmusic.release();
Log.e("Fehlersuche", "onPause");
super.onPause();
}
```

Restarting the app with the help of <Run> should no longer display any error in the Logcat window; it should show only our Logcat designations.

Logcat 02-25 13:04:36.194	28803-28803/com.greendog.example.webapp	E/Fehlersuche :
onCreate 02-25 13:04:36.434	28803-28803/com.greendog.example.webapp	E/Fehlersuche :
onResume 02-25 13:04:36.785	28803-28803/com.greendog.example.webapp	E/Fehlersuche :
onPause 02-25 13:04:39.027	28803-28803/com.greendog.example.webapp	E/Fehlersuche :
onResume 02-25 13:04:49.597	28803-28803/com.greendog.example.webapp	E/Fehlersuche :
onPause 02-25 13:04:56.454	28803-28803/com.greendog.example.webapp	E/Fehlersuche :
onResume		

onCreate starts the activity.

onPause is activated whenever a user clicks on the Wiki button or exits the app.

onResume is activated when a user clicks the Back button from the Wiki page.

If you are interested, you can now change the telephone or the emulator (CTRL + F11) from horizontal to vertical format a few times and monitor its consequence in the Logcat.

onCreate is called with every change. This means that each change in the orientation restarts the activity and starts the music from the beginning.

This might be OK or even desired for a few apps. However, if you do not want to restart the activity in case of an orientation change, you can prevent this using an entry in the AndroidManifest.xml file.

Add the following Activity element for the Baskerville activity:

```
<activity
android:name="com.greendog.example.webapp.Baskerville"
android:configChanges="orientation|screenSize|uiMode"android:label="@string/
baskervilles" >
<intent-filter>
<action android:name="android.intent.action.MAIN" />
<category android:name="android.intent.category.LAUNCHER" />
</intent-filter>
</activity>
```

After saving and running the app using <Run>, onCreate should appear only once in the Logcat - at the beginning.

Preventing the orientation change is common especially for games. In such a case, you can use the AndroidManifest.xml file to define the orientation for respective activities (e.g. portrait or landscape).

Sample entry:

android:screenOrientation="portrait"

Both attributes configChanges and screenOrientation for the <activity> element now only have 2 of the several possible attributes. However, these 2 are the ones that are most frequently used. You can get a list of all possible attributes when you write "android:". The available attributes are shown at the latest after writing the colon.

A description of attributes is given on:

http://developer.android.com/guide/topics/manifest/activity-element.html

The second activity of the app: Tasty

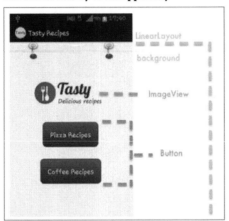

The content to be displayed comprises two external websites/web apps. Instead of using a typical web server, we will use two free alternatives, namely Google's AppEngine and GitHub Pages. AppEngine is used for a series of different "backends" for Android apps. The Pizza Recipes page is received from AppEngine and is stored there as a Java web app. For information regarding this popular technique, visit:

https://developers.google.com/appengine/docs/java/gettingstarted/introduction

Both pages were created using HTML5 and mobile jQuery and are thus optimised for the display on mobile devices.

Creating the Tasty.java Java class

Right click and select the New option on the package name to display the following context menu (Android Studio Version 0.4.6 or higher):

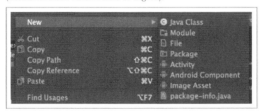

Two options, namely Java Class and Activity, are available to add a new class. The difference between the two - Java Class creates an empty class and Activity create a Java class with the code of the selected template.

In our case, it makes sense to select the Activity option and the Blank Activity template. Then fill in the fields accordingly:

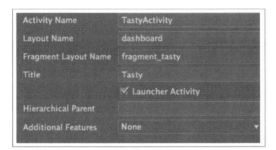

This results in a "Hello World" activity that does not do anything different than the dashboard.xml layout file, which we will create now, to begin with.

When you click on the launcher, Android Studio sets an activity element for this activity in the AndroidManifest.xml file with the MAIN and LAUNCHER attributes, whose icons are created on the Home screen.

```
<activity
android:name="com.greendog.example.webapp.TastyActivity"
android:label="@string/title_activity_tasty" >
<intent-filter>
<action android:name="android.intent.action.MAIN" />
<category android:name="android.intent.category.LAUNCHER" />
</intent-filter>
</activity>
```

Creating a new icon In order to display a separate icon for the TastyActivity on the Home screen, you can use the built-in "Image Asset" wizard to create an customised icon for this activity.

Right click on the "app folder" or the package name -> New -> Image Asset

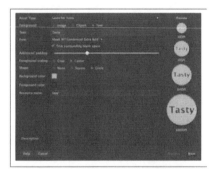

Here you can let your creativity loose. Allocate a new name as the 'Resource name' to ensure that the default App icon is not overwritten. You can now add a new attribute in the AndroidManifest file:

```
<activity
android:name="com.greendog.example.webapp.TastyActivity"
android:label="@string/title_activity_tasty"
android:icon="@drawable/tasty" >
<intent-filter>
<action android:name="android.intent.action.MAIN" />
<category android:name="android.intent.category.LAUNCHER" />
</intent-filter>
</activity>
```

The layout for the app

The app opens a start-up page from which both alternatives can be selected. Start-up pages, which provide all app alternatives, are also known as the dashboard. The figure shows the layout of a dashboard. To create a new layout file, right click on

layout -> New -> Layout resource file

and name the file, e.g. dashboard.xml. Two (2) images are required for the layout. The first image, recipenote.png, is added as a "background" to the LinearLayout. The second image, logo.png, is placed in an ImageView using buttons. Images can either be copied to the drawable/ folder or alternatively in the drawable-mdpi/ folder.

For the button, define an xml file as described in the DinoQuiz chapter and store it in drawable/.

I have named the file for buttons button2.xml. The simplest option is to copy the xml file of DinoQuiz and add it to drawable/. You can then change the colours as per your choice using the colour palette on the left side.

All resources are now ready and we can create the dashboard.xml layout file.

```xml
<?xml version="1.0" encoding="utf-8"?>
<LinearLayout
xmlns:android="http://schemas.android.com/apk/res/android"
android:id="@+id/dashboard"
android:layout_width="match_parent"
android:layout_height="match_parent"
android:background="@drawable/receipenote"
android:gravity="center_vertical|center_horizontal"
android:orientation="vertical" >


<ImageView
android:id="@+id/imageView1"
android:layout_width="wrap_content"
android:layout_height="wrap_content"
android:layout_marginBottom="40dp"
android:src="@drawable/logo"
android:contentDescription="@string/logo"/>

<Button
android:id="@+id/button1"
android:layout_width="wrap_content"
android:layout_height="wrap_content"
android:layout_marginBottom="30dp"
android:onClick="openPizza"
android:background="@drawable/button2"
android:textColor="@android:color/white"
android:text="@string/pizza" />

<Button
android:id="@+id/button2"
android:layout_width="wrap_content"
android:layout_height="wrap_content"
android:onClick="openCoffee"
android:background="@drawable/button2"
android:textColor="@android:color/white"
android:text="@string/coffee" />
</LinearLayout>
```

The upper button should open the link for the "Pizza Recipes" and therefore contains:

```
android:onClick="openPizza"
```

The lower button should open the link for "Coffee Recipes" and therefore contains:

```
android:onClick="openCoffee"
```

Adding the methods for opening the web apps for TastyActivty

Under the onCreate method, add both methods for opening both web apps:

```
@Override
protected void onCreate(Bundle savedInstanceState) {
super.onCreate(savedInstanceState);
setContentView(R.layout.dashboard);
}
     // open first button: pizza recipes located on github pages
public void openPizza(View v) {
String url = "http://janebabra.github.io/veggipizza//";
Intent intent = new Intent(Intent.ACTION_VIEW);
intent.setData(Uri.parse(url));
startActivity(intent);
}
     // open second button: coffee recipes located on AppEngine
public void openCoffee(View v) {
String url = "http://coffee-recipes-pro.appspot.com/";
Intent intent = new Intent(Intent.ACTION_VIEW);
intent.setData(Uri.parse(url));
startActivity(intent);
}
```

Starting the app creates two icons on the Home screen:

Both activities can now be directly started from the Home screen independently.

The third activity: Roundball

We will again integrate web contents in this app, but in a different manner than that used in the last activity. In the last activity, we have called the internal Android browser to load external websites. When contents are sent to the internal Android browser, the Android browser takes over the complete control.

Instead of this, we will use a web kit in this activity. The web kit gives us the option of defining our own browser; the contents can, but must not, use the entire space in a layout. The layout area, where the contents need to be displayed, is set in a widget named WebView.

The web kit provides a series of ON - OFF buttons similar to JavaScript = true or false.

Roundball a game created in JavaScript and built on the "LIME" GameEngine. A demo version of this game can be downloaded from the LIME's website.

Web resources, which are to be stored locally in the app, are stored in a folder called assets/. To create this folder, right click on the main/ folder, select -> New -> Directory and specify "assets" as the folder name. Here you can later copy the HTML/ JavaScript files belonging to the game.

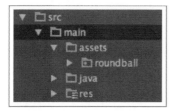

Creating the Roundball activity

Similar to the last example, we will again create an activity using the Blank Activity template, click on LAUNCHER and create a customised icon. We will first need to import a web kit in order to use it. We will need to add the WebView. Then create a variable for the WebView to be created afresh.

```
package com.greendog.example.webapp;
import android.os.Bundle; import android.app.Activity; import
android.webkit.WebView;
public class Roundball extends Activity {

WebView myWebView;
@Override
protected void onCreate(Bundle savedInstanceState) {
super.onCreate(savedInstanceState);
setContentView(R.layout.activity_roundball);
```

The code for loading the game in the WebView is given below. R.id.webView1 does not exist at the moment. This becomes the ID that will add to the WebView in the activity_roundball layout file.

```
setDomStorageEnabled(true);
```

Many JavaScript games like this one and most LIME games are built on DOM instead of Canvas. setJavaScriptEnabled(true); naturally, JavaScript has to be enabled for a JavaScript game.

```
loadUrl("file:///android_asset/roundball/roundball.html");
```

Finally, we will call the Start HTML file for starting the game. The android_asset specifications correspond to the real assets directory.

```
WebView myWebView;

@Override
protected void onCreate(Bundle savedInstanceState) {
super.onCreate(savedInstanceState);
setContentView(R.layout.activity_roundball);
myWebView = (WebView) findViewById(R.id.webView1);
myWebView.getSettings().setDomStorageEnabled(true);
myWebView.getSettings().setJavaScriptEnabled(true);
myWebView.loadUrl("file:///android_asset/roundball/roundball.html");
    }
  }
```

The activity_roundball.xml layout file

The layout file comprises a widget, the WebView and its ID is webView1 that is called from the Java class.

```
<RelativeLayout
xmlns:android="http://schemas.android.com/apk/res/android"
xmlns:tools="http://schemas.android.com/tools"
android:layout_width="match_parent"
android:layout_height="match_parent"
tools:context=".MainActivity" >
<WebView
android:id="@+id/webView1"
android:layout_width="match_parent"
android:layout_height="match_parent"
android:layout_alignParentLeft="true"
android:layout_alignParentTop="true" />  </RelativeLayout>
```

When you start the app on the telephone or the emulator, it shows 3 icons so that the game can be directly launched.

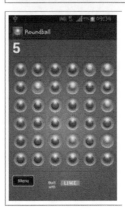

HTML CODE IN STRINGS.XML AND TEXTVIEW

The fourth example shows how you can include the HTML code/ text in a TextView. HTML texts are relatively frequently added to the info pages of an app. The advantages are obvious. In the TextView, you can use the same methods for design and formatting elements as the ones used in a website. In addition, the text can include clickable links that lead to other apps in Google Play Store.

Our objective is to create the following **info page**:

It should be called from the Info button of the ActionBar similar to the one we have created in the First project chapter.

This also means that we will add the Info page to the "My Application" project from the First project chapter. We therefore need to close our current project and open the My Application project.

We need to do three things:

1. Provide resources for the Info page

2. Create the layout for the Info page

3. Linking the Info button with the Info page through programming

Resources for the Info page

Add the text for the Info page in the strings.xml file. The HTML code is encapsulated in:

```
<![CDATA[Inhalt]]>
```

This prevents Android from trying to interpret the HTML code tags as Android code. For the above Info page, the entry in the strings.xml file must look as follows:

```
<string name="about_text"><![CDATA[
<p><h1>Android lernen am Beispiel</h1></p>
<p><h2>Android Programmierung mit Android Studio</h2></p>
Copyright © 2014 Barbara Hohensee<br /> </center> <br/>
<b>This app is licensed under Creative Commons Attribution License 3.0
<a href="http://creativecommons.org/licenses/by/3.0/">
creativecommons.org/licenses/by/3.0/</b></a> <br />
<p>The App has the following properties:</p> - TextView, <br /> - ScrollView,
<br /> - textHTML, <br /> - WindowSizeHelper, <br /> - ActionBar, and more
<br /> <br />
The book blog: <br />
<a href="http://google-android-studio.blogspot.com">http://google-android-
studio.blogspot.com/</a>
<br /> <br />
Source code on GitHub:  <br /> <a href="https://github.com/
janebabra">https://github.com/janebabra </a> <br />
 <br /> ]]></string>
```

The layout for the Info page

We will create a new layout file as per the known method. For this example, I have named it info.xml. The layout only has a TextView that is enclosed with a ScrollView. The background colour was defined in the ScrollView such that it fills the entire screen.

The text from strings.xml is added to the TextView (text_target) using the Java class (AboutActivity).

```xml
<?xml version="1.0" encoding="utf-8"?>
<ScrollView
xmlns:android="http://schemas.android.com/apk/res/android"
android:layout_width="match_parent"
android:layout_height="match_parent"
android:layout_marginBottom="8dp"
android:layout_marginTop="8dp"
android:background="#fff0d490">

<TextView
android:paddingLeft="15dp"
android:paddingRight="15dp"
android:paddingTop="7dp"
android:paddingBottom="7dp"
android:id="@+id/text_target"
android:layout_width="match_parent"
android:layout_height="wrap_content"/>
</ScrollView>
```

Linking the Info button with the Info page through programming

The definitions for the Info button of the ActionBar were already included in the main.xml file under menu/.

In order to make the button clickable, the placeholder of onOptionsItemSelected(MenuItem item) is replaced with the real code in MainActivity.

```
@Override
public boolean onOptionsItemSelected(MenuItem item) {
switch (item.getItemId()) {                    case R.id.action_about:
Intent intent = new Intent(this, AboutActivity.class);
startActivity(intent);
return true;                case R.id.action_settings:
Intent intent2 = new Intent(this, AboutActivity.class);
startActivity(intent2);
return true;                default:
return super.onOptionsItemSelected(item);
}
}
```

case R.id.action_about: is used for calling the Info page.

The new intent calls *AboutActivity* which is responsible to display the Info page on the screen.

Structure of AboutActivity

```
...
import android.app.Activity;
import android.os.Bundle;
import android.text.Html;
import android.text.method.LinkMovementMethod; import
android.widget.TextView;
public class AboutActivity extends Activity {
@Override
protected void onCreate(Bundle savedInstanceState) {
super.onCreate(savedInstanceState);
setContentView(R.layout.info);
        WindowSizeHelper.adjustWindowSize(this);

TextView v = (TextView) findViewById(R.id.text_target);
v.setText(Html.fromHtml(getString(R.string.about_text)));
v.setMovementMethod(LinkMovementMethod.getInstance());
v.setLinksClickable(true);
}
}
```

import android.text.Html; is the new thing in this activity

This import enables converting the HTML code in strings.xml into text.

```
import android.text.method.LinkMovementMethod;
```
This import is required if you want to add clickable links in the text.

```
TextView v = (TextView) findViewById(R.id.text_target);
v.setText(Html.fromHtml(getString(R.string.about_text)));
v.setMovementMethod(LinkMovementMethod.getInstance());
v.setLinksClickable(true);
```

The TextView retrieves the text from the about_text variable in strings.xml and sets it to the position of the TextView (text_target) in the info.xml layout file. setMovementMethod and setLinksClickable allow exiting the TextView and opening the link in a new window.

```
WindowSizeHelper.adjustWindowSize(this);
```

The use of WindowSizeHelper is optional. The app functions even without this refinement. If you do not want to use WindowSizeHelper, you comment the line: // WindowSizeHelper.adjustWindowSize(this);

WindowSizeHelper's task is to reduce the size of the window in which the Info page is displayed. As a result, the Info page looks as if it has been customised for this size. The code of the WindowSizeHelper.java Java class can be universally used for all possible apps.

The seventh project: Survey form

Contents of this chapter:

- Text fields (EditText)
- Text watcher for strings
- Weights
- Conditions
- Catching errors with Try/ catch
- Share intent

I now leave it up to the experienced readers to create a new project containing one view (1 Java class and its associated layout file). Only one image needs to be provided as a resource; it can be optionally stored in the drawable/ or drawable-mdpi/ folder.

The target form should look as follows:

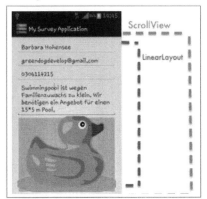

The form has 4 EditText fields, i.e. the fields that can be filled in, and a "Send button" in the form of a bathtub duck that is included in a LinearLayout. A ScrollView encloses the LinearLayout.

The EditText fields that are used here are of a special form of EditText that are known as TextFields widgets. These can be added in the layout using the drag-and-drop method.

The advantage of text fields over simple EditText fields is that the matching keyboard layouts are shown when filling the form. The numeric keyboard is shown for the "Phone" text field; the alphabet keyboard layout is shown for the "Person Name" text field, etc.

The "Name" text field is used for entering the name. The text field contains the following code in the *activity_main.xml* layout file:

```
<EditText
android:id="@+id/name"
android:layout_width="match_parent"
android:layout_height="wrap_content"
android:ems="10"
android:hint="@string/your_name"
android:inputType="textPersonName" >
```

android:ems="10" indicates that the width of the field should be 10 "m".You can use the android:hint attribute to store a hint text as a background in a field; this hint text disappears as soon as a user starts writing.

The language of the keyboard does not depend on the language of the form, but on the language that is set as a default language in the telephone/emulator.

The "E-mail" text field is used for entering the email address. The text field contains the following code in the *activity_main.xml* layout file:

```
<EditText
android:id="@+id/email"
android:layout_width="match_parent"
android:layout_height="wrap_content"
android:ems="10"
android:hint="@string/your_email_address"
android:inputType="textEmailAddress" />
```

The "Phone" text field is used for entering the email address. The text field contains the following code in the *activity_main.xml* layout file:

```
<EditText
android:id="@+id/phone"
android:layout_width="match_parent"
android:layout_height="wrap_content"
android:ems="10"
android:hint="@string/your_phone"
android:inputType="phone" />
```

The "Multiline text" text field is used for entering the name. The text field contains the following code in the *activity_main.xml* layout file:

```
<EditText
android:id="@+id/comments"
android:layout_width="match_parent"
android:layout_height="wrap_content"
android:layout_weight="5"
android:ems="10"
android:hint="@string/comments_and_feedback"
android:inputType="textMultiLine"
android:minLines="3" />
```

The andoid:minLine="3" attribute allows more space to the comments field in the form that is not yet filled.

The image button for sending the form contains the following code in the activity_main.xml layout file:

```
<ImageButton
android:id="@+id/imageButton1"
android:layout_width="wrap_content"
android:layout_height="wrap_content"
android:layout_gravity="right"
android:layout_weight="10"
android:adjustViewBounds="true"
android:contentDescription="@string/submit"
android:onClick="processForm"
android:src="@drawable/duck"
android:visibility="invisible" >
</ImageButton>
```

The android:layout_weight attribute can be used to influence spaces in the layout. If a value is not defined for the "weight" attribute, its default value is 1. If its value is 10, the button has 10 times more space than, e.g. lines for the name.

If android:adjustViewBounds="true", the image button fills the space optimally. All widgets can contain an attribute to make it visible or invisible. The android:visibility="invisible" attribute thus makes the button invisible when the form is called.

In the Java file, you can define when to make the button visible through programming.

Editing an existing Java class (MainActivity.java)

The description of the source code was added as comments // comment
You can manually add the required imports or wait for Android Studio automatically executing the import or suggesting the import.

```
 ... import android.app.Activity;
import android.content.Intent;
import android.os.Bundle;
import android.text.Editable;
import android.text.TextWatcher;
import android.util.Log;
import android.view.Menu;
import android.view.View;
import android.view.animation.Animation;
import android.view.animation.AnimationUtils;
import android.widget.EditText;


// Instead of only "extends Activity", implements
// TextWatcher is additionally added here. As a result, programming of
TextWatcher is simplified.

public class MainActivity extends Activity implements TextWatcher {
     private static final String TAG = "MainActivity";

// A variable is defined for each of the input fields
private EditText mName;
private EditText mPhone;
private EditText mEmail;
private EditText mComment;


@Override
protected void onCreate(Bundle savedInstanceState) {
super.onCreate(savedInstanceState);
setContentView(R.layout.activity_main);
 // The connection with the fields in the layout is established
mName = (EditText) findViewById(R.id.name);
mPhone = (EditText) findViewById(R.id.phone);
mEmail = (EditText) findViewById(R.id.email);
mComment = (EditText) findViewById(R.id.comments);
// In this example, the task of TextWatcher is to monitor the field of
comments (mComment)
//
mComment.addTextChangedListener(this);
 }
// When TextWatcher is used, 3 methods are required:
// onTextChanged, beforeTextChanged, afterTextChanged
// We have used only afterTextChanged
```

```java
@Override
public void onTextChanged(CharSequence s,
int start, int before, int count) {
}
@Override
public void beforeTextChanged(CharSequence s,
int start, int count,
int after) {
}
@Override
public void afterTextChanged(Editable s) {
String comments = s.toString();
// getString returns a Java string pointer to a resource string
String duck = getString(R.string.duck);
// Logcat notification
Log.d(TAG, "Checking for " + duck);
// Checked whether something was added to comments
// The text is converted to small case
// The text "duck" is not included in the text
boolean valid = comments.length() > 0 && comments.toLowerCase().indexOf(duck)
== -1;          View view = findViewById(R.id.imageButton1); // The text in
comments does not contain the word "duck"
// Send button VISIBLE is set          boolean isVisible =
view.getVisibility() == View.VISIBLE;
if (isVisible == valid) {
return;
} // if-else condition for starting animation          Animation anim;
if (valid) {
// Creates a new animation object
anim = AnimationUtils.makeInAnimation(this, true);
view.setVisibility(View.VISIBLE);              } else {
// Creates a new animation object
anim = AnimationUtils.makeOutAnimation(this, true);
view.setVisibility(View.INVISIBLE);
}
// Starts animation
view.startAnimation(anim);
}

@Override
public boolean onCreateOptionsMenu(Menu menu) {
// Inflate the menu; this adds items to the action bar if it is present.
getMenuInflater().inflate(R.menu.main, menu);
return true;
}      public void processForm(View duck) {
simpleShareExample();      }
public void simpleShareExample() {

// The simplest form to send a notification ....
Intent i = new Intent(Intent.ACTION_SEND);
i.setType("text/plain");
i.putExtra(Intent.EXTRA_TEXT, "What a wonderful app!");
startActivity(i);          } }
```

Note regarding animation: It can be viewed only on the emulator or tablet. The keyboard hides animation on the telephone. Note regarding emulator: If you want to send an email, you first need to set up an e-mail account on the emulator.

SHARE INTENTS

- ACTION_SEND
- ACTION_VIEW
- ACTION_SENDTO

ACTION_SEND

If ACTION_SEND is used, Android searches for suitable applications from the installed programmes and shows this as a list. The user can select any programme from the list.

ACTION_VIEW

ACTION_VIEW can be used to restrict the choice for the user and to define that the notification is sent via SMS. Sample code:

```
public void simpleShareExample() {
// Send as SMS ....
String comments = mComment.getText().toString();
String phone = mPhone.getText().toString();
Intent intent = new Intent(Intent.ACTION_VIEW);
intent.setData(Uri.fromParts("sms", phone, null));
intent.putExtra("sms_body", comments);
try {
startActivity(intent);
} catch (Exception ex) {
Log.e(TAG, "Could not send message", ex);
}
```

ACTION_SENDTO

ACTION_SENDTO can be used to restrict the choice for the user and to define that the notification is sent via an email. Sample code:

```
public void simpleShareExample() {
// Send as email....
String comments = mComment.getText().toString();
String email = mEmail.getText().toString();
String phone = mPhone.getText().toString();
String name = mName.getText().toString();
String message = name + " says.. " + comments;
if (phone.length() > 0) {
message = message + ":" + phone;
}


if (email.length() > 0) {
message = message + "Email:" + email;
}
Intent emailIntent = new Intent(Intent.ACTION_SENDTO);
emailIntent.setData(Uri.fromParts("mailto", "feedback@myapp.somewhere...",
null));
emailIntent.putExtra(Intent.EXTRA_SUBJECT, "important news");
emailIntent.putExtra(Intent.EXTRA_TEXT, message);
if (emailIntent.resolveActivity(getPackageManager()) == null) {
Toast.makeText(getApplicationContext(),
"Please configure your email client!", Toast.LENGTH_LONG)
.show();
} else {
startActivity(Intent.createChooser(emailIntent, "Please choose your email
app!"));
 }
```

For more information about ACTION_SEND, visit Google's Developer site:

http://developer.android.com/reference/android/content/Intent.html#ACTION_SEND

The eighth project:

Graphics, drawing and animation

http://developer.android.com/training/building-graphics.html

In Android, graphics, images and text can be displayed in 3 different views:

- View + canvas (2D)
- SurfaceView + canvas (2D)
- OpenGL (2D + 3D)

DRAWING IN A VIEW

You can use View.onDraw () if our application does not demand memory-consuming system resources or fast image rates. This might be a case in a drawing programme similar to the one we will create in the next chapter.

If the drawing is based on the view, the size is determined by the views. The canvas used serves as a screen on which objects such as points, lines, texts and images from the drawable/ folder are drawn. The following code draws line.

```
class DrawView extends View {
Paint paint = new Paint();
public DrawView(Context context) {
super(context);
paint.setColor(Color.BLUE);
}
@Override
public void onDraw(Canvas canvas) {
super.onDraw(canvas);
canvas.drawLine(10, 10, 90, 10, paint);
}
 }
```

For drawing operations, Android uses the four fundamental classes:

Canvas -> the screen used for drawing

Paint -> it is the tool used for drawing (colours, brush size)

Drawable -> graphic objects such as circles, rectangles and images, but no text

Bitmap -> it is result of actually drawn pixels

Coordinate system

```
0,0

y

|
|
|
+------------------------> x
```

The coordinates of the top-left corner on the screen are x = 0 and y = 0. canvas.drawLine has 4 coordinates: startx, starty, stopx, stopy

Colours

paint.setColor() can accept colour definitions in different formats. In the above example, the colour was directly specified as a name: (Color.BLUE). This method can be used to specify some colours such as GREEN, BLACK, WHITE, RED, BLUE, CYAN, DKGRAY, GRAY, LTGRAY, MAGENTA, YELLOW.

The hexadecimal colour scheme is another option to specify colours. The format is: 0xff808080. Specifications range from 0 to f, i.e. 0,1,2,3,4,5,6,7,8,9,a,b,c,d,e,f. The first two digits indicate the transparency. f indicates no transparency and 0 indicates complete transparency. The next 6 digits are colours like red, green and blue. Two groups are used for the specification.

Hexadecimal code of the blue colour: 0xff000080.

Example for drawing in a view

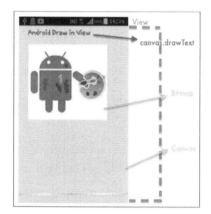

Sample source code: MyDrawApplication

```
package com.greendog.example.mydrawapplication.app;
import android.app.Activity;
import android.content.Context;
import android.graphics.Bitmap;
import android.graphics.BitmapFactory;
import android.graphics.Canvas;
import android.graphics.Color;
import android.graphics.Paint;
import android.os.Bundle;
import android.view.View;
import android.view.Window;
public class ViewGraphicsActivity extends Activity {
@Override
public void onCreate(Bundle savedInstanceState) {
super.onCreate(savedInstanceState);
requestWindowFeature(Window.FEATURE_NO_TITLE);
setContentView(new MyView(this));       }       class MyView extends View {
public MyView(Context context) {
super(context);
}

@Override
public void onDraw(Canvas canvas) {
Paint paint = new Paint();
paint.setColor(Color.RED);
paint.setTextSize(30);
paint.setAntiAlias(true);
canvas.drawColor(Color.YELLOW);
canvas.drawText("Android Draw in View", 40, 40, paint);
Bitmap image = BitmapFactory.decodeResource(getResources(),
R.drawable.android);
canvas.drawBitmap(image, 40, 80, null);
}
}
}
```

We will need the following imports to create our own view:

```
import android.content.Context;
import android.view.View;
import android.view.Window;
```

The following is imported for the "Draw" activities:

```
import android.graphics.Bitmap;
import android.graphics.BitmapFactory;
import android.graphics.Canvas;
import android.graphics.Color;
import android.graphics.Paint;
```

It is common practice to remove the title bar from draw apps or games

```
requestWindowFeature(Window.FEATURE_NO_TITLE);
```

The app does not have an xml layout file; the view is used instead:

```
setContentView(new MyView(this));
```

The canvas is created using the method

```
public void onDraw(Canvas canvas)
```

Paint: A new "paint tool" is first created using Paint paint = new Paint();. We will the add attributes like colour and brush thickness, etc. paint and canvas have a large number of attributes that are shown in Android Studio as soon as a point is defined.

The image integrated here is called android.jpg and it is stored in the drawable/ folder. A bitmap that is drawn on the canvas must first be retrieved from the folder using BitmapFactory and then decoded. Only then it can be drawn with canvas.drawBitmap.

Drawing in the SurfaceView

http://developer.android.com/reference/android/view/SurfaceView.html

SurfaceView example

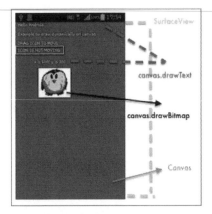

We will first create a new activity called MySurfaceViewActivity. As in the
last example, an xml layout is not used for the display on the screen; the
layout is created in the Java class.

```
public class MySurfaceViewActivity extends Activity {
@Override
public void onCreate(Bundle savedInstanceState) {
super.onCreate(savedInstanceState);
requestWindowFeature(Window.FEATURE_NO_TITLE);
setContentView(new MySurface(this));
}
}
```

We will first create an "inner class" that extends SurfaceView and implements
SurfaceHolder.callback.

This automatically includes 3 methods:

1.surfaceChanged

2.surfaceCreated

3.surfaceDestroyed

These form the life cycle of the SurfaceView.

```
class MySurface extends SurfaceView implements SurfaceHolder.Callback {
@Override
public void surfaceChanged(SurfaceHolder holder, int format, int width, int
height) {
}
@Override
public void surfaceCreated(SurfaceHolder holder) {
}
@Override
public void surfaceDestroyed(SurfaceHolder holder) {
}
}
```

The *MySurface* class created above is supplemented with Callback methods and calls SecondThread (thread) inside the respective constructor.

```
class MySurface extends SurfaceView implements SurfaceHolder.Callback {

private SecondThread thread;
//Initial position for the image
private int x = 100;
private int y = 200;
public MySurface(Context context) {
super(context); getHolder().addCallback(this);
thread = new SecondThread(getHolder(), this);
}

@Override
public void surfaceChanged(SurfaceHolder holder, int format, int width, int
height) {
}

@Override
public void surfaceCreated(SurfaceHolder holder) {
thread.setRunning(true); thread.start();
}

@Override
public void surfaceDestroyed(SurfaceHolder holder) {
boolean retry = true; thread.setRunning(false);
while (retry) { try { thread.join(); retry = false; }
catch (InterruptedException e) {
} } } }
```

The SecondThread class is created with essential parameters for Surface and SurfaceHolder.

```
class SecondThread extends Thread {
private SurfaceHolder surfaceHolder;
private MySurface mySurface;
private boolean _run = false;
public SecondThread(SurfaceHolder surfaceHolder, MySurface mySurface) {
this.surfaceHolder = surfaceHolder;    this.mySurface = mySurface;
}
public void setRunning(boolean run) {
_run = run;
}

@Override
public void run() {
Canvas c;  while (_run) {
c = null; try {
c = surfaceHolder.lockCanvas(null);
synchronized (surfaceHolder) {
mySurface.onDraw(c);
}
}
finally { if (c != null) { surfaceHolder.unlockCanvasAndPost(c);
} }
} } }
```

We will now use the canvas object for the graphics

```
public void onDraw(Canvas canvas) {
Paint paint = new Paint();
paint.setColor(Color.WHITE);
paint.setTextSize(20);
paint.setAntiAlias(true);
canvas.drawColor(Color.BLUE);
canvas.drawText("Hello Android", 10, 20, paint);
Bitmap image = BitmapFactory.decodeResource(getResources(),
R.drawable.ic_launcher);
//The image is rendered using the parameters of x and y
//Values for x and y are inferred from touch events
canvas.drawBitmap(image, x, y, null);
}
```

The listener for touch events.

```
@Override
public boolean onTouchEvent(MotionEvent event) {
if (event.getAction() == MotionEvent.ACTION_MOVE) {
x = (int) event.getX(); y = (int) event.getY(); }
return true;
}
```

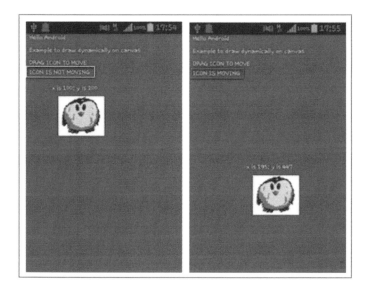

To be able to start the activity from the Home screen, we will again add the MAIN and LAUNCHER attributes in the AndroidManifest.xml file.

```
<activity
android:name="com.greendog.example.mydrawapplication.app.MySurfaceViewActivity"
android:label="@string/title_activity_surfaceview" >
<intent-filter>
<action android:name="android.intent.action.MAIN" />
<category android:name="android.intent.category.LAUNCHER" />
</intent-filter>
</activity>
```

OPENGL ES

OpenGL ES is a compact and powerful low-level 3D rendering standard for embedded systems. This standard is based on the known OpenGL graphics standard and was introduced by the Khronos Group in Siggraph 2002. The existing OpenGL standard was shortened and adapted such that it conserves the limited resources on embedded systems. In Android, Version 2.0 of the OpenGL ES standard is completely implemented; this is based on the OpenGL standard 1.3. Some functions of the 1.1 standard have also been integrated. Using the 2.0 standard is however recommended at present.

OpenGL ES offers better performance in 2D in the form of view and SurfaceView. Therefore, it is partially used in 2D games. OpenGL ES is primarily used in 3D games, Google Maps v2 and Augment Reality. OpenGL ES requires the following entry in the AndroidManifest.xml file

```
<uses-feature
android:glEsVersion="0x00020000"
android:required="true"/>
```

Android provides a series of different animations. One of the most commonly used animation is illustrated below; it is called Tween.

Tween animation

The Tween animation requires parameters such as

- start value
- end value
- size
- time duration
- rotation angle

etc., to be able to used in a specific object. Android has a separate class for the type of animation; it is called Animation. An instance of the Animation class is created and the loaded information from the xml file is written into an object/a variable (animation in this case).

```
Animation animation = AnimationUtils.loadAnimation(getApplicationContext(),
R.anim.myanimation);
```

The xml files for the definition of the animation are stored in res/ in the anim/ folder. This folder is normally not created by default; hence, we need to create it manually.

The Animation class contains the following methods:

No.	Method	Description
1	start()	This method starts the animation
2	setDuration()	This method sets the duration of the animation
3	getDuration()	This methods contains the time information of setDuration
4	end()	This method ends the animation
5	cancel()	This method cancels the animation

Example of using the animation with startAnimation() in an image object.

```
ImageView image1 = (ImageView)findViewById(R.id.imageView1);
image.startAnimation(animation);
```

Zoom-In animation

The sample code shows the contents of an animation xml file for enlarging (zoom in) an object.

```
<set xmlns:android="http://schemas.android.com/apk/res/android">
<scale xmlns:android="http://schemas.android.com/apk/res/android"
android:fromXScale="0.5" android:toXScale="3.0" android:fromYScale="0.5"
android:toYScale="3.0" android:duration="5000" android:pivotX="50%"
android:pivotY="50%" >
</scale>
</set>
```

The fromXScale and fromYScale parameters define the start points and the toXScale and toYScale parameters define the end points. The duration parameter defines the time. The pivotX and pivotY parameters define the centre from which the animation starts.

Sample project

For this project, we can either reuse the "My Application" project or create a new project using the blank template (Hello World) plus the ActionBar and add the ActionBar to the project as described in the "First project" chapter.

We will first create the anim/ folder in res/.

Copy any image for the subsequent animation in the drawable/ or drawable-mdi folder.

An ImageView for the image is added to the activity_main.xml layout file:

```
<RelativeLayout
xmlns:android="http://schemas.android.com/apk/res/android"
xmlns:tools="http://schemas.android.com/tools"
android:layout_width="match_parent"
android:layout_height="match_parent"
android:gravity="top"
android:paddingBottom="@dimen/activity_vertical_margin"
android:paddingLeft="@dimen/activity_horizontal_margin"
android:paddingRight="@dimen/activity_horizontal_margin"
android:paddingTop="@dimen/activity_vertical_margin"
tools:context=".MainActivity" >

<ImageView android:id="@+id/imageView1"
android:layout_width="wrap_content"
android:layout_height="wrap_content"
android:layout_alignParentTop="true"
android:layout_centerHorizontal="true"
android:layout_marginTop="179dp"
android:src="@drawable/flying_pinguin" />
</RelativeLayout>
```

For the **zoom-in animation**, we will create the zoomin.xml file in the res/anim folder

(New -> Animations resource file) with the following contents:

```xml
<?xml version="1.0" encoding="utf-8"?>
<set xmlns:android="http://schemas.android.com/apk/res/android">
<scale xmlns:android="http://schemas.android.com/apk/res/android"
android:fromXScale="0.5" android:toXScale="3.0" android:fromYScale="0.5"
android:toYScale="3.0" android:duration="5000" android:pivotX="50%"
android:pivotY="50%" >
</scale>

<scale xmlns:android="http://schemas.android.com/apk/res/android"
android:startOffset="5000" android:fromXScale="3.0" android:toXScale="0.5"
android:fromYScale="3.0" android:toYScale="0.5" android:duration="5000"
android:pivotX="50%" android:pivotY="50%" >
</scale>
</set>
```

For the **clockwise animation**, we will create the clockwise.xml file with the following contents in the res/anim folder:

```xml
<?xml version="1.0" encoding="utf-8"?>
<set xmlns:android="http://schemas.android.com/apk/res/android">
<rotate xmlns:android="http://schemas.android.com/apk/res/android"
android:fromDegrees="0" android:toDegrees="360" android:pivotX="50%"
android:pivotY="50%" android:duration="5000" >
</rotate>

<rotate xmlns:android="http://schemas.android.com/apk/res/android"
android:startOffset="5000" android:fromDegrees="360" android:toDegrees="0"
android:pivotX="50%" android:pivotY="50%" android:duration="5000" >
</rotate>
</set>
```

For the **zoom-out animation**, we will create the zoomout.xml file with the following contents in the res/anim folder:

```xml
<?xml version="1.0" encoding="utf-8"?>
<set xmlns:android="http://schemas.android.com/apk/res/android"
android:interpolator="@android:anim/accelerate_interpolator" >
<alpha
android:fromAlpha="0" android:toAlpha="1" android:duration="2000" > </alpha>
<alpha
android:startOffset="2000" android:fromAlpha="1" android:toAlpha="0"
android:duration="2000" >
</alpha>
</set>
```

Animations should be called via the **Options menu**. We will add the following to res/menu/main.xml:

```xml
<menu xmlns:android="http://schemas.android.com/apk/res/android"
xmlns:greendog="http://schemas.android.com/apk/res-auto>
<item android:id="@+id/rotate360"
android:icon="@android:drawable/ic_menu_rotate"
android:title="@string/rotate_String"
greendog:showAsAction="always" />

<item android:id="@+id/zoomInOut"
android:icon="@android:drawable/ic_menu_zoom"
android:title="@string/zoom_In_Out"
greendog:showAsAction="ifRoom"/>

<item android:id="@+id/fadeInOut"
android:icon="@android:drawable/ic_delete"
android:title="@string/fade_String"
greendog:showAsAction="never/>
</menu>
```

We can inherit the names for menu entries as they are or write our own names in res/values/string.xml:

```xml
<?xml version="1.0" encoding="utf-8"?>
<resources>
<string name="app_name">Animation</string>
<string name="action_settings">Settings</string>
<string name="hello_world">Hello world!</string>
<string name="zoom_In_Out">Zoom In/Out</string>
<string name="rotate_String">Clockwise/Anti Clockwise</string>
<string name="fade_String">Fade In/Out</string>
</resources>
```

Establishing a connection in the Java file

The following code is added to the *MainActivity.java* file for calling the menu.

```java
package com.example.animation;
import com.example.animation.R;
import android.os.Bundle;
import android.app.Activity;
import android.view.Menu;
import android.view.MenuItem;
import android.view.animation.Animation;
import android.view.animation.AnimationUtils;
import android.widget.ImageView;

public class MainActivity extends Activity {
@Override protected void onCreate(Bundle savedInstanceState) {
super.onCreate(savedInstanceState);
setContentView(R.layout.activity_main);
}


@Override
public boolean onCreateOptionsMenu(Menu menu) {
// Inflate the menu; this adds items to the action bar if it is present.
getMenuInflater().inflate(R.menu.main, menu); return true;
}

public boolean onOptionsItemSelected(MenuItem item) {
super.onOptionsItemSelected(item); switch(item.getItemId()) {
case R.id.zoomInOut: ImageView image =
(ImageView)findViewById(R.id.imageView1);
Animation animation = AnimationUtils.loadAnimation(getApplicationContext(),
R.zoomin);
image.startAnimation(animation); return true; case R.id.rotate360: ImageView
image1 = (ImageView)findViewById(R.id.imageView1);
Animation animation1 = AnimationUtils.loadAnimation(getApplicationContext(),
R.anim.clockwise); image1.startAnimation(animation1);
return true;
case R.id.fadeInOut: ImageView image2 =
(ImageView)findViewById(R.id.imageView1);
Animation animation2 = AnimationUtils.loadAnimation(getApplicationContext(),
R.anim.zoomout);
image2.startAnimation(animation2);
return true;
}
return false;
} }
```

Time to test the animation. A screenshot of the app on a table is given below.

The app starts.

The icon in the ActionBar for the Clockwise animation was clicked.

The ninth project: Fragments

WHAT ARE FRAGMENTS

With the introduction of Android tablets and Android Version 3.0 (HONEYCOMB), a new layout concept named Fragments was added to the SDK. The original idea was to utilise the screen of a table in a better manner using Fragments that display two "screens" at a time.

1. Activity with 2-pane fragment layout

When the app is run on a tablet, a relevant fragment is opened whenever one of the elements from the list is selected. A new activity is not called. On a telephone, screens are displayed one after the other.

Without Fragments, screens are displayed on all devices, which use the same structure, one after the other irrespective of the screen size. You can take into different screen sizes into account by defining other dimensions and font sizes in the values-sw600dp and values-sw720dp-land folders; the structure however remains the same.

Activity with ListView

Activity with details for the "my tv family" element

Activity with details for the Meine Familie (my family) element

In addition to the aforementioned 2-pane fragment layout, 1-pane fragment layout can also be used. For the latter, there is only one screen that contains one or more fragments that can be changed during the runtime of the activity.

From the technical point of view, fragments are linked with an activity which controls these fragments. Thus, there is a dependency between an activity and its fragments.

Similar to activities, fragments also have a life cycle. The following figure shows the structure and the links of the fragment life cycle with the activity life cycle: 2-pane fragment layouts are illustrated in this chapter

Project: Homecoming/ Class Reunion

The time of folding photo books to add achievements such as "My house", "My boat", "My car" etc. is in the past. The time from today is specified using a Smartphone and in our case a specific Android app.

The app starts with the activity: ItemListActivity and waits for the decision whether the code should be executed for a telephone or a tablet.

Finally, the telephone and the tablet show the contents using the ItemDetailFragment fragment.

Fragments are replaced using the "replace" option. You can use the "add" option to add fragments and the "remove" option to remove them. In all cases, commit(); must be included to execute the command.

The ItemDetailFragment class defines which contents need to be displayed where and includes a TextView and an ImageView.

```
@Override
public View onCreateView(LayoutInflater inflater, ViewGroup container,
                         Bundle savedInstanceState) {
View rootView = inflater.inflate(R.layout.fragment_item_detail, container,
false);

// Show the text in a TextView.
        if (mItem != null) {

((TextView)rootView.findViewById(R.id.item_detail)).setText(Html.fromHtml(mIt
em.text));

        }
// Show the image in an ImageView
((ImageView) rootView.findViewById(R.id.image_view))
             .setImageResource(mItem.image),
        return rootView;
    }
  }
```

The *fragment_item_detail.xml* layout file is constructed like any other layout file.

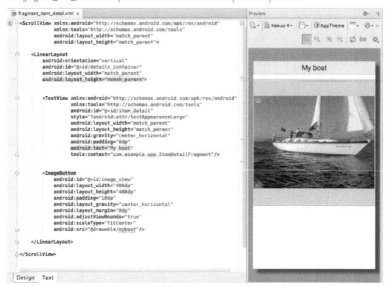

The *activity_item_detail.xml* layout file that is coupled with ItemDetailActiviy (telephone) contains only one FrameLayout so that it can include the contents from the fragment_item_detail.xml file.

ItemDetailAcitvity determines which fragment needs to be added at which location.

```
if (savedInstanceState == null) {
// Create the detail fragment and add it to the activity
// using a fragment transaction.
Bundle arguments = new Bundle();
arguments.putString(ItemDetailFragment.ARG_ITEM_ID,
getIntent().getStringExtra(ItemDetailFragment.ARG_ITEM_ID));
ItemDetailFragment
fragment = new ItemDetailFragment();
fragment.setArguments(arguments);
getSupportFragmentManager().beginTransaction()
.add(R.id.item_detail_container, fragment)
.commit();
}       }
```

A view of the *refs.xml* file shows how it is linked with *ItemListActivity*.

```
<resources>
<!--      Layout alias to replace the single-pane version of the layout with a
two-pane version on large screens. For more on layout aliases, see:
http://developer.android.com/training/multiscreen/
screensizes.html#TaskUseAliasFilters      -->

<item type="layout" name="activity_item_list">@layout/activity_item_twopane
</item>
</resources>
```

If you right-click on "*activity_item_list*" and then on **Find Usage**, the following window will be displayed and you can see the link between *refs.xml* and *activity_item_list.xml*.

Creating the 2-pane layout (master/ detail flow)

A new project with minimum requirement SDK 11 and support mode: Fragments are created. Fragments can also be created for apps, which use versions lower than Android 3.0, using the support-v4 library. This is however not applicable to the special layout form of the master/ detail flow.

The master / detail flow is selected in the next step

The master/ detail flow is a template that creates the complete structure of the app. We must only add our contents.

The template created the structure that we have just discussed.

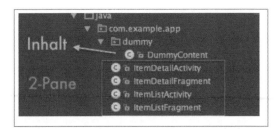

In addition to the discussed 2-pane structure, the DummyContent Java class is available, wherein the contents for the table of contents (ListView) and the detail view are defined.

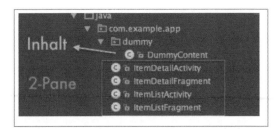

Entries can be saved as text ("Mein Haus" (my house)) as well as resource (R.drawable.myhouse).

Text entries are defined as String (public String title;)

Resource entries are defined as **int** (public int image;)

Entries from [2] are transferred

Finally, allocate a self-defined and self-explanatory name

The template can be used to create a series of different apps. The second example shows how we can use this template to retrieve web contents.

Project: German TV on-the-go

A small number of German TV broadcasters who offer the Internet TV so that the live streaming of news headlines can be viewed outside Germany as well.

We simply need to edit 3 files to adapt the master / detail flow template as per desired web contents: DummyContent.java

New entries for the table of contents and the detail view

```
addItem(new DummyItem("1", "Das Erste", "http://live.daserste.de/"));
addItem(new DummyItem("2", "ZDF", "http://wdmpa.zdf.de/mediathek"));
addItem(new DummyItem("3", "Sat1", "http://www.sat1.de"));
addItem(new DummyItem("4", "RTL Now", "http://www.rtl.de/"));
addItem(new DummyItem("5", "Kabel1", "http://www.kabeleins.de"));
addItem(new DummyItem("6", "n-tv", "http://www.n-tv.de"));
addItem(new DummyItem("7", "Tagesschau", "http://www.tagesschau.de/multimedia/livestreams/"));
addItem(new DummyItem("8", "VOX", "http://www.vox.de"));
addItem(new DummyItem("9", "n-tv", "http://www.n-tv.de"));

}

private static void addItem(DummyItem item) {
    ITEMS.add(item);
    ITEM_MAP.put(item.id, item);
}

/**
 * A dummy item representing a piece of text.
 */
public static class DummyItem {
    public String id;
    public String title;
    public String website;


    public DummyItem(String id, String title, String content ) {
        this.id = id;
        this.title = title;
        this.website = content;
```

ItemDetailFragment.java

The required WebView must be defined here along with its options

```
@Override
public View onCreateView(LayoutInflater inflater, ViewGroup container,
        Bundle savedInstanceState) {
    View rootView = inflater.inflate(R.layout.fragment_item_detail, container, false);

    // Show the dummy content in a WebView
    if (mItem != null) {
        ((WebView) rootView.findViewById(R.id.item_detail)).getSettings().setJavaScriptEnabled(true);
        ((WebView) rootView.findViewById(R.id.item_detail)).getSettings().setDomStorageEnabled(true);
        ((WebView) rootView.findViewById(R.id.item_detail)).setWebChromeClient(new WebChromeClient());
        ((WebView) rootView.findViewById(R.id.item_detail)).loadUrl(mItem.website);
    }

    return rootView;
```

fragment_item_detail.xml

The layout file for web contents must include a WebView

```xml
<WebView xmlns:android="http://schemas.android.com/apk/res/android"
         android:id="@+id/item_detail"
         android:layout_width="match_parent"
         android:layout_height="match_parent">

</WebView>
```

The area around fragments is spacious. Examples shown here indicate the first step with which we can develop a series of apps. However, there is lot to learn as far as options and variations of fragment-based layouts are concerned.

Normally, you can decide whether and when you want to use fragments. However, there are a few exceptions where the developers are forced to work with fragments. One of these is the so-called PreferenceScreen that is explained in the next chapter. Another example is Google Maps v2 that is included in the Google Play Service SDK chapter.

Using fragments, especially the 2-pane layouts, is also interesting when you want to develop for Google TV apps. The app that we have just developed can run on a television set equipped with Google TV without any changes.

Good starting point for further reading: http://developer.android.com/guide/components/fragments.html An interesting, but rather complex example of fragments is given in the samples of the SDK. This example is called HoneycombGallery.

Developing for Google TV

WHAT IS GOOGLE TV?

Google TV is a specially adapted Android version that runs on television sets. A standard Android version was extended with properties such as channel switching. Android on television sets appears with the known apps that are available on a telephone or tablet.

The Google TV Android version cannot be downloaded. The source code is provided only to OEM producers in order to integrate Google TV in external Google TV sticks, boxes or television sets.

Google TV is often called Smart TV, especially by TV manufacturers who do not want to sell their devices as "Android" TV. Google TV is available on 3 different devices:

As an HDMI stick whose size is equal to that of a cigarette lighter and that can be plugged into the HDMI port of a television set.

As a set-up box (buddy box) that is connected to the television set using an HDMI cable.

As an integrated part of the television set.

When Google TV was introduced for the first time in 2010, it was not more than a device with which one could stream movies from Internet without leaving the television set. It is thus comparable with Apple TV or the Chromecast stick.

In the meanwhile, the Android version and even the hardware in which it is installed have been further developed. An example of the equipment such as HDMI sticks available in Internet shops:

2 GB RAM, 1.8 Ghz quad-core CPU and 16 GB Flash Nand Memory for approximately 50 €.

Thanks to several apps running on Google TV, it can be combined with a wireless keyboard/ mouse and can be used as a second computer.

A range of programmes could be installed on on Google TV:

•   Movie apps

•   Gallery for images

•   Music players

•   Internet browser

•   Email

•   Calendar

•   Facebook

•   Twitter

- Google+
- Office
- Google Drive
- Dropbox
- E-book readers
- Games

When you can use Google TV as a computer, the spectrum of apps that the developers can create for this platform is also extended. Those, who are looking out for a niche area where the competition is not as severe as in the telephone market, have probably already found there future field of operation. Developing for Google TV

Android Studio automatically offers a work environment to develop apps for telephones, tablets and Google TV. Additional plugins or similar are not required. The information on the Google site is obsolete. Google TV examples:

Google TV Remote https://code.google.com/p/google-tv-remote/

Google TV sample code https://code.google.com/p/googletv-android-samples/

Unfortunately, there are only a few examples and all of them are for Eclipse. At present, some projects cannot be easily converted and run in Android Studio. Having a look at the source code, especially Java classes, is still recommended.

"Google TV Remote" is an example that I have converted and its source code for Android Studio is available.

Google TV Remote is interesting because not all external Google TV devices are equipped with a remote control. The buyer can invest in an additional remote control or alternatively install the remote control app on the telephone.

Here is the link to the Google Play Store:

https://play.google.com/store/apps/details?id=com.google.android.apps.tvremote

The source code for Google's TV remote as Android Studio project:

https://github.com/janebabra/gtv/tree/master/google-tv-remote

Black Jack example

The Black Jack example will help you in learning about the so-called "Second Screen".

The Second Screen is a screen that shows the actions carried out using telephone apps. In the Black Jack game, the Second Screen is the card table.

The game is installed on telephones of players.

If you have developed an app, you want to run and test it before offering it for downloading on the Google Play Store.

Similar to apps for telephones and tablets, the adb program is responsible for running the app either of the emulator or on a connected device.

When the adb runs the app on a device (telephone), it is normally connected via USB. If you have a free USB port on your Google TV, you can proceed exactly as if you are connecting a telephone.

However, there is an option to switch over the adb to Wifi and install the app on Google TV in a wireless mode.

Switching over the adb to a WiFi connection

The USB connection is a default connection for the adb. Proceed as follows to switch over from USB to Wifi:

Connect the telephone with the computer via USB

Open a terminal window and navigate to the platform-tools folder using the cd command

Switch to Wifi using one of the following commands

adb tcpip 5555 or ./adb tcpip 5555 (Mac, Linux)

```
mr-macs-macbook:platform-tools mrmac$ ls
NOTICE.txt              api                     source.properties
adb                     fastboot                systrace
mr-macs-macbook:platform-tools mrmac$ ./adb tcpip 5555
* daemon not running. starting it now on port 5037 *
* daemon started successfully *
restarting in TCP mode port: 5555
```

Configuration in Google TV

Search for the IP address in Settings -> About -> Status

In this example, this IP address is 192.168.0.103

Terminal window

Enter the following command in the terminal window to connect to Google TV:

```
adb connect 192.168.0.103
```

```
mr-macs-macbook:platform-tools mrmac$ ./adb connect 192.168.0.103
* daemon not running. starting it now on port 5037 *
* daemon started successfully *
connected to 192.168.0.103:5555
```

Android Studio

If you now click on "Run" in Android Studio, Google TV should appear in the list of the Choose Device window

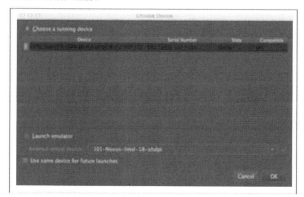

Similar to apps that were tested on the telephone, you can see all events of running Google TV in the Logcat window. You can naturally take screenshots of your app.

Special features in Google TV

The resolution of Google TV is either 720p or 1080p at present.

720p means:

1280 x 720 px screen size in pixel

tvdpi is the qualifier for the image folder, e.g. drawable-tvdpi

The screen density is 213 dp

The qualifier for the layout folder is large, e.g. layout-large

1080p means:

1920 x 1080 px screen size in pixel

xhdpi is the qualifier for the image folder, e.g. drawable-xhdpi

The screen density is 320 dp

The qualifier for the layout folder is large, e.g. layout-large

The TV is always in the landscape format.

Colours on the TV appear differently than those on telephones or tablets. Therefore, testing on the correct Google TV and not only on the emulator is extremely important.

The following setting is recommended for tests that you want to conduct on the emulator:

"10.1 WXGA (Tablet) (1280 x 800: mdpi) "

The tenth project: Preferences

http://developer.android.com/guide/topics/ui/settings.html Android contains the following mechanisms for saving and receiving the data:

- Preferences
- SQLite3 databases
- Files
- Network

WHAT ARE PREFERENCES

SharedPreferences are suitable for saving the application data permanently. It is normally used to store the status information and common data between multiple activities of an application. A key/value pair is associated with every entry. The key is a String and the value must be a primitive data type. Android has three different types of preferences:

- Activity-level preferences
- Application-level preferences
- SharedPreferences, beyond the app limit, with other apps

The following data types are allowed in SharedPreferences:

- Boolean values
- Float values
- Integer values
- Long values
- String values

Project: Pinguine auf dem Eis (penguin on ice)

Download the example and open it in Android Studio:

GitHub:

https://github.com/janebabra/Android_lernen_am_Beispiel/tree/master/Eispinguine

Test the app on the emulator or telephone before using the Preferences page. The app starts

The app starts with 2 penguins that are rotating on their own ice surface.

Moving the penguin with the finger You can move the penguins on the ice surface using your finger and mark traces on the ice that describe the path of movements. Penguins remain at the position where you have moved them using your finger and they keep rotating. The "no name" message is displayed next to these penguins since we have not assigned any name until now.

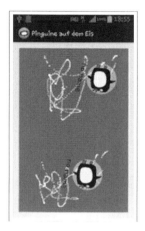

Setting the Preferences page

For this example, only two of the sub-classes of Preferences from the Preference class are used; these are CheckBoxPreference and EditTextPreference. For a complete list, visit:

http://developer.android.com/reference/android/preference/Preference.html

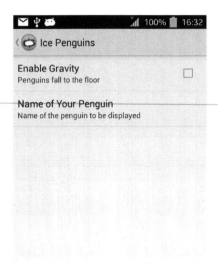

Creating a layout file

To create an xml layout file, right-click on the res/ folder,

Select **New**

and then **Android resource file**

In the next window, assign the name, select XML as resource type and confirm with <OK>.

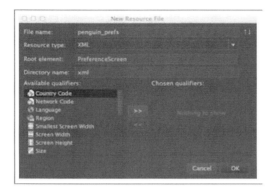

A folder called *xml/*, which contains the layout file that we have just created, should appear in the file structure.

Enter the code for both value pairs:

For **CheckBoxPrefence**, create the following key/ value pair:

Key: gravity

Value: Enable Gravity

and a description in the Summary field: Penguins fall to the floor

The **gravity** value is saved using SharedPreferences so that it can be read later by the *PeguinView.java* activity. The type of CheckBoxPreferences is always Boolean, i.e. either true or false. The entry for the CheckBoxPreference section in the *penguin_prefs.xml* file would look like the following:

```
<?xml version="1.0" encoding="utf-8"?>
<PreferenceScreen
xmlns:android="http://schemas.android.com/apk/res/android" >
<CheckBoxPreference
android:title="Enable Gravity"
android:key="gravity"
android:summary="Penguins fall to the floor"/>
</PreferenceScreen>
```

For **EditTextPrefence**, create the following key/ value pair:

Key: name

Value: Enable Name of Your Penguin

and a description in the Summary field: Name of the penguin to be displayed

The name value is also saved using SharedPreferences so that it can be read later by the *Peguin View.java* activity.

The type of EditTextPreferences is always String.

The entry extended with EditTextPreference in the *penguin_prefs.xml* file would look like the following:

```
<?xml version="1.0" encoding="utf-8"?>
<PreferenceScreen
xmlns:android="http://schemas.android.com/apk/res/android" >
<CheckBoxPreference
android:title="Enable Gravity"
android:key="gravity"
android:summary="Penguins fall to the floor"/>
<EditTextPreference
android:summary="Name of the penguin to be displayed"
android:key="name"
android:title="Name of Your Penguin"/>
</PreferenceScreen>
```

Creating a Java class for preferences

Right-click on ->

New - > Activity

to create a new activity and name it, e.g. *SettingsActivity.java*.

There are normally three different versions for the Java code:

Java code for Android up to 3.0

Java code for Android 3.0

Java code examples

Java code for Android up to 3.0

```
public class SettingsActivity extends PreferenceActivity {
```

```
@Override
public void onCreate(Bundle savedInstanceState) {
super.onCreate(savedInstanceState);
// Load the preferences from an XML resource
        addPreferencesFromResource(R.xml.penguin_prefs);
}
}
```

Java code for Android 3.0 and higher

```
public static class SettingsFragment extends PreferenceFragment {
@Override
public void onCreate(Bundle savedInstanceState) {
super.onCreate(savedInstanceState);
// Load the preferences from an XML resource
addPreferencesFromResource(R.xml.penguin_prefs);
}
...
 }
```

Java code for all Android versions

```
public class SettingsActivity extends PreferenceActivity {
@Override
protected void onCreate(Bundle savedInstanceState) {
super.onCreate(savedInstanceState);
// Display the fragment as the main content.
getFragmentManager().beginTransaction()
.replace(android.R.id.content, new SettingsFragment())
 .commit();
 } }
```
The third variant is used in the example given here. We must first determine the API version of the device to be able to respond to different API versions:

if (Build.VERSION.SDK_INT < Build.VERSION_CODES.HONEYCOMB) {

go to code for Android older than Android 3.0 }

else {

go to code for Android 3.0 or higher}

The related code for SettingsActivity is:

```
package greendog.movingpenguins;
import android.annotation.TargetApi;
import android.app.Activity;
import android.app.Fragment;
```

```java
import android.app.FragmentTransaction;
import android.os.Build;
import android.os.Bundle;
import android.preference.PreferenceActivity;
import android.preference.PreferenceFragment;
import android.util.Log;
import android.view.LayoutInflater;
import android.view.View;
import android.view.ViewGroup;
public class SettingsActivity extends PreferenceActivity {
@Override
protected void onCreate(Bundle savedInstanceState) {
super.onCreate(savedInstanceState);
if (Build.VERSION.SDK_INT < Build.VERSION_CODES.HONEYCOMB) {
showPreferencesPreHoneycomb();
} else {
showPreferencesFragmentStyle(savedInstanceState);
}       }
@SuppressWarnings("deprecation")
private void showPreferencesPreHoneycomb() {
Log.d("Android Version", "Pre-Honeycomb!");
addPreferencesFromResource(R.xml.penguin_prefs);
}
/* From here, only for Android Version 3.0 or higher */
@TargetApi(Build.VERSION_CODES.HONEYCOMB)
private void showPreferencesFragmentStyle(Bundle savedInstanceState) {
if (savedInstanceState == null) {
FragmentTransaction transaction = getFragmentManager()
.beginTransaction();
Fragment fragment = new MyPreferencesFragment();
transaction.replace(android.R.id.content, fragment);
transaction.commit();
}       }
@TargetApi(Build.VERSION_CODES.HONEYCOMB)
public static class MyPreferencesFragment extends PreferenceFragment {
@Override
public void onAttach(Activity activity) {
super.onAttach(activity);
Log.d("Android Version", "Honeycomb or higher");
}
@Override
public View onCreateView(LayoutInflater inflater, ViewGroup container,
Bundle savedInstanceState) {
this.addPreferencesFromResource(R.xml.penguin_prefs);
return super.onCreateView(inflater, container, savedInstanceState);
}
}       ; }
```

It is not difficult to understand that SettingsActivity does not anything other than providing the Settings screen. However, a reaction to changes, which were clicked or written here, is still missing.

We need to modify the activity that actually shows the changes on the screen. In our example, this activity is *PenguinView.java*.

Defining the SharedPreference variables

We will define the following 3 variables in the *PenguinView.java* activity:

private String mPenguinName;

private boolean mEnableGravity;

private SharedPreferences mPrefs;

Contents of the name of EditTextPreferences key are stored in **mPenguinName**. Contents of the gravity of CheckBoxPreferences key are stored in **mEnableGravity**. The **mPrefs** variable is a connection channel between SharedPreferences and keys.

The Settings screen does not contain any OK button or similar. You only need to enter your changes and exit the screen using the Back button of the telephone. Use onSharedPreferenceChanged, which receives every change immediately, to ensure that the PenguinView.java activity can respond immediately to changes without restarting the app.

```
@Override
public void onSharedPreferenceChanged(SharedPreferences p, String key) {
// Simple but inefficient:
// For each preference item that changes we will read all of the preferences
again
mPenguinName = mPrefs.getString("name", "no name"); mEnableGravity =
mPrefs.getBoolean("gravity", true);
}
mPenguinName = mPrefs.getString("name", "no name");
```

"name" is the key from EditTextPreferences and "no name" is the presetting.

 mEnableGravity = mPrefs.getBoolean("gravity", true);

"gravity" is the key from CheckBoxPreferences and true is the presetting. Integrate preferences as settings in the App menu

The minimum requirement to make the Settings screen accessible is to integrate it in the Options menu so that the Settings page can be called using the Menu button of the telephone.

The menu/main.xml file for the Options menu contains the entry for settings by default. We will now modify it as follows:

```
<menu
xmlns:android="http://schemas.android.com/apk/res/android" >
```

```
<item
android:id="@+id/action_settings"
android:title="@string/action_settings"
android:icon="@android:drawable/ic_menu_preferences"
app:showAsAction="ifRoom" />
</menu>
```

This can be activated in MainActivity in the already prepared onOptionsItemSelected section along with the specification of the intent, i.e. the activity with which the page should be started

```
@Override
public boolean onOptionsItemSelected(MenuItem item) {
int id = item.getItemId(); if(id == R.id.action_settings) {
Intent i = new Intent(this,SettingsActivity.class);
startActivity(i);
return true;
}
return super.onOptionsItemSelected(item);
}
```

Until now, the Settings screen was accessible only via the Menu button of the telephone.

Modern form pages such as Settings must be called using the ActionBar. In cases where the app runs in the full-screen mode, i.e. when the ActionBar is not visible, you must use the option to call the pages using the Menu button of the telephone.

Accessing the Settings screen via ActionBar

An entry in the *AndroidManifest.xml* file is extended with the ActionBar theme. We must do this for all activities in which we want to make the ActionBar and its menus visible.

```
<activity
android:name=".MainActivity"
android:label="@string/app_name"
android:theme="@style/Theme.AppCompat.Light" >
<intent-filter>
<action android:name="android.intent.action.MAIN" />
<category android:name="android.intent.category.LAUNCHER" />
</intent-filter>
</activity>
```

An entry for the appcompat compatibility library must be included in the *build.gradle* file.

build.gradle

```
dependencies {
compile 'com.android.support:support-v4:+'
compile 'com.android.support:appcompat-v7:+'
}
```

The new look with the ActionBar icon for the Settings page

Another refinement could be adding *SettingsActivity* to a "Home button". We first need to activate the ActionBar for this purpose.

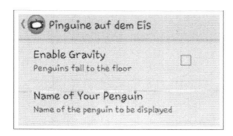

Adding in *SettingsActivity*

The Home button functions in PreferenceActivity only in case of HONEYCOMB or higher. This is a bug in AppCompat that is used as a support library. The problem is that "extends PreferenceActivity" must be included here for the functioning of our SettingsActivity. The getActionBar() or getSupportActionBar() call must however be accessed only in extends ActionBarActivity.

```
public class SettingsActivity  extends PreferenceActivity {
@Override
public boolean onOptionsItemSelected(MenuItem item) {
        switch (item.getItemId()) {
            case android.R.id.home:
                // app icon in action bar clicked; go home
                Intent intent = new Intent(this, MainActivity.class);
                intent.addFlags(Intent.FLAG_ACTIVITY_CLEAR_TOP);
                startActivity(intent);
                return true;

            default:
                return super.onOptionsItemSelected(item);
        }
    }

@Override
protected void onCreate(Bundle savedInstanceState) {
if(Build.VERSION.SDK_INT >= Build.VERSION_CODES.HONEYCOMB)
getActionBar().setDisplayHomeAsUpEnabled(true);
        super.onCreate(savedInstanceState);
if (Build.VERSION.SDK_INT < Build.VERSION_CODES.HONEYCOMB) {
showPreferencesPreHoneycomb();
} else {
showPreferencesFragmentStyle(savedInstanceState);
 }
}
```

Starting the app on a telephone with Android 2.3.6 does not show any ActionBar. We need to return to the primary activity using the Back button like before.

The eleventh project: SQLite database

http://developer.android.com/training/basics/data-storage/index.html This chapter is not intended at imparting the database or SQL knowledge, but to explain how a database of the SQL type, that is called SQLite 3 in Andros, can be integrated into an app. Fundamental knowledge acquired through working with databases such as MS SQL or MySQL is advantageous in this case.

WHAT IS SQLITE?

SQLite is a database system that, unlike MySQL, comes without a server. SQLite comprises a collection of libraries that provide the database functionality. Android provides an interface through which the app can access a SQLite database. An auxiliary class called SQLiteOpenHelper is required to integrate a SQLite database into an app. The resultant database class is an instance of SQLiteDatabase. The resultant auxiliary class provides the four basic operations, namely Create, Read, Update and Delete. These are also called CRUD, i.e. Create, Read (Query), Update and Delete. Methods for CRUD are listed below: insert()It adds one or more rows in the database.

query()It retrieves the rows that fulfil the criteria entered by you.

update()It updates one or more rows that fulfil the criteria entered by you.

delete()It deletes one or more rows that fulfil the criteria entered by you.

The following example includes:

- Create a database
- Create a table
- Add values in the table
- Retrieve values from the table
- Display the result data as ListView
- Delete values from the table

Create a database

```
sampleDB = this.openOrCreateDatabase(SAMPLE_DB_NAME, MODE_PRIVATE, null);
```

This opens the SAMPLE_DB_NAME database if it already exists, or it is created and then opened. The MODE_PRIVATE parameter gives authorisations for this app. The MODE_WORLD_WRITABLE and MODE_WORLD_READABLE parameters are used if you want to access other apps in the database.

If a database has been successfully created, it is stored under /data/data/Paketname/databases/datenbankname.db

Create a table

```
sampleDB.execSQL("CREATE TABLE IF NOT EXISTS " +
SAMPLE_TABLE_NAME +
" (LastName VARCHAR, FirstName VARCHAR," +
" Country VARCHAR, Age INT(3));");
```

Add values in the table

```
sampleDB.execSQL("INSERT INTO " +
SAMPLE_TABLE_NAME +
" Values ('Makam','Sai Geetha','India',25);");
```

Retrieve values from the table

```
Cursor c = sampleDB.rawQuery("SELECT FirstName, Age FROM " +
SAMPLE_TABLE_NAME +
" where Age > 10 LIMIT 5", null);
if (c != null ) {
if  (c.moveToFirst()) {
do { String firstName = c.getString(c.getColumnIndex("FirstName"));
 int age = c.getInt(c.getColumnIndex("Age"));
 results.add("" + firstName + ",Age: " + age);
}while (c.moveToNext());
}
}
```

Display the result data as ListView

```
this.setListAdapter(new ArrayAdapter<String>
      (this,android.R.layout.simple_list_item_1,results));
```

Delete values from the table

```
finally {
if (sampleDB != null)
sampleDB.execSQL("DELETE FROM " + SAMPLE_TABLE_NAME);
sampleDB.close();
 }
```

Creating a sample project

There are no special requirements. The project comprises only one Java class. There is no xml layout file. The layout is created inside the Java class. The data from the database is shown in a ListView. For this, the activity must contain extends ListActivity and the import android.app.ListActivity;

```
import android.app.ListActivity;
public class CRUDonDB extends ListActivity {
```

The layout is created with

```
this.setListAdapter(new ArrayAdapter<String>(this,
      android.R.layout.simple_list_item_1,results));
```

After creating the database, all data is added using a cursor (cursor):

```
Cursor cursor = sampleDB.rawQuery("SELECT PuppyName, Sex, BreedName, Age FROM
"
      SAMPLE_TABLE_NAME +            " where Age > 5 LIMIT 5", null);
 if (cursor != null ) {
 if  (cursor.moveToFirst()) {
do {
String firstName = cursor.getString(cursor.getColumnIndex("PuppyName"));
String breed = cursor.getString(cursor.getColumnIndex("BreedName"));
String sex = cursor.getString(cursor.getColumnIndex("Sex"));
int age = cursor.getInt(cursor.getColumnIndex("Age"));
results.add("" + firstName + ",Sex: " + sex + ", " + breed + ", Age: " +
age);
}while (cursor.moveToNext());
}
}
```

The data is sent to the ArrayList (results).

```
ArrayList<String> results = new ArrayList<String>();
```

The only task of this database is to display existing data from the database. Thus, it does not support interactive session with users. Most apps use sqlite NUR to display data.

The complete code for the project:

```
package com.greendog.example.app; import android.app.ListActivity;
import android.database.Cursor;
import android.database.sqlite.SQLiteDatabase;
import android.database.sqlite.SQLiteException;
import android.os.Bundle;
import android.util.Log;
import android.widget.ArrayAdapter;
import java.util.ArrayList;
public class CRUDonDB extends ListActivity {
private final String SAMPLE_DB_NAME = "myDogsDb";
private final String SAMPLE_TABLE_NAME = "dogs";
/** Called when the activity is first created. */

@Override
public void onCreate(Bundle savedInstanceState) {
super.onCreate(savedInstanceState);
ArrayList<String> results = new ArrayList<String>();
SQLiteDatabase sampleDB = null;
try {
sampleDB = this.openOrCreateDatabase(SAMPLE_DB_NAME, MODE_PRIVATE, null);
ampleDB.execSQL("CREATE TABLE IF NOT EXISTS " +            SAMPLE_TABLE_NAME +
" (PuppyName VARCHAR, BreedName VARCHAR," +            " Sex VARCHAR, Age
INT(3));");
sampleDB.execSQL("INSERT INTO " +            SAMPLE_TABLE_NAME +            "
Values ('Jenny','Mix','female',15);");            sampleDB.execSQL("INSERT INTO
" +            SAMPLE_TABLE_NAME +            " Values ('Theo','Terrier','male',
9);");
sampleDB.execSQL("INSERT INTO " +            SAMPLE_TABLE_NAME +            "
Values ('Jacky','Tibet Terrier','female',8);");
Cursor cursor = sampleDB.rawQuery("SELECT PuppyName, Sex, BreedName, Age FROM
" +            SAMPLE_TABLE_NAME +            " where Age > 5 LIMIT 5", null);

if (cursor != null ) {
if  (cursor.moveToFirst()) {
do {
String firstName = cursor.getString(cursor.getColumnIndex("PuppyName"));
String breed = cursor.getString(cursor.getColumnIndex("BreedName"));
String sex = cursor.getString(cursor.getColumnIndex("Sex"));
int age = cursor.getInt(cursor.getColumnIndex("Age"));
results.add("" + firstName + ",Sex: " + sex + ", " + breed + ", Age: " +
age);
}while (cursor.moveToNext());
}
```

```
}
this.setListAdapter(new ArrayAdapter<String>(this,
android.R.layout.simple_list_item_1,results));
                   } catch (SQLiteException se ) {
Log.e(getClass().getSimpleName(), "Could not create or Open the database");
} finally {
if (sampleDB != null)
sampleDB.execSQL("DELETE FROM " + SAMPLE_TABLE_NAME);
sampleDB.close();
        }
    }
}
```

BONUS PROJECT: PHOTO DIARY

Source code on GitHub:

https://github.com/janebabra/Android_lernen_am_Beispiel/tree/master/PhotoDiary

Photo Diary is an app that saves the SQLite3 database for storing diary entries comprising a photo and the text for the description of the incident. Unlike the introductory example, the user creates database entries in the database. The database is thus empty at the beginning. Database entries can be created afresh or deleted. Photo Diary is not only a classical example of a database structure that required interactivity, but is also a good example for creating a prototype. A prototype is required to ensure the users can create an app with a different objective with minimal changes, e.g. holiday diary, new puppy diary, inventory for household contents insurance, collection of miniature characters, etc.

An app becomes considerably complex when interactivity is required.

The database of Photo Diary

When databases become complex or need to handle a large data volume, the work on the database may sometimes be carried out outside Android Studio.

How is the list of entries displayed on the screen?

As in the last example, entries are collected in an ArrayList. This ArrayList is called myList and comprises a HashMap.

The private void createList() method is used to display the ListView and to make individual entries clickable.

$$myList = new ArrayList<HashMap<String, Object>>();$$

Accessing the database in the emulator via a terminal

In the terminal window, switch to the path of platform tools

cd /Applications/Android Studio.app/sdk/platform-tools

The platform-tools folder contains the **adb** program. The adb program is used to establish the contact with the running emulator and to open a shell.

The command for adb:

In Windows: adb In Linux

Mac OS: ./adb

Check whether the emulator is accessible

```
./adb devices
```

List of devices attached

emulator-5554 device

Establishing a connection for the emulator at the Shell level

```
./adb -s emulator-5554 shell #
```

Establishing a connection with the desired database

```
# sqlite3 /data/data/com.greendog.PhotoDiary/databases/photodiary.db SQLite version 3.6.22
```

Enter ".help" for instructions Enter SQL statements terminated with a ";" sqlite>

Viewing the database contents

sqlite> .tables BILD

android_metadata sqlite> select * from bild; 1|/mnt/sdcard/photobook/ ALB_20140306_175836.jpg|test |wer weiss|hier ||06.03.2014-17:59||

sqlite>

Exporting a SQLite database

The database can be exported to the File Explorer of the DDMS. This is required to work on it in the SQLite browser. The edited database can then be re-imported using the File Explorer.

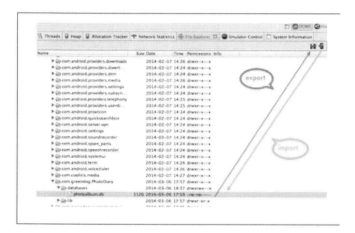

After exporting the database, programs such as sqlite or SQLite browser can be used to work on the database.

https://www.sqlite.org/sqlite.html

SQLite browser

SQLite browser is a program that is not included in Android Studio. It can be used to modify the database structure and contents. The program can be downloaded for Windows, Mac and Linux.

http://sourceforge.net/projects/sqlitebrowser/

Google Play Service SDK

The Google Play Service SDK is a new library that includes various services. These services include Google Maps Android API v2, Google+, Google In-app Billing v3 and Google Cloud Messaging.

In order to use the Google Play Service SDK, we first need to download the "Google Play services" package from Tools using the SDK Manager. The library is integrated into the project by using an entry in build.gradle. The aforementioned services can now be used in the Android project.

The following example shows the integration of Google Maps API v2.

Creating an SHA-1 fingerprint

An SHA-1 fingerprint (release or debug certificate) needs to be created to request for a Google Map v2 API key.

Command to get a debug certificate

Windows:

keytool -list -v -keystore "C:_user_nameandroid.keystore" -alias androiddebugkey -storepass android -keypass android

Mac OS X and Linux:

```
keytool -list -v -keystore ~/.android/debug.keystore -alias androiddebugkey -
storepass android -keypass android
```

Command to get a release certificate

```
keytool -list -keystore your-keystore-name
```
The your-keystore-name placeholder is replaced with the complete path and the name of your release keystore. Once you press Enter, the system asks you to enter your 'keystore password'. A list of all aliases that you have created and an SHA-1 row for each alias are then displayed. Copy the SHA-1 fingerprint so that it is available when the Google Map v2 API key is requested by the 'Google API Console'.

Creating a project in the Google API Console

You can access the Google API Console from: https://code.google.com/apis/console

From the Drop-Down menu on the left side, select <create> and assign the desired project name. Now select <Services> from the menu under your project name; a list of selectable APIs is displayed. Activate the API called "Google Maps Android API v2" by setting the button next to it to ON.

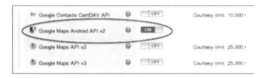

Return to the menu that you have just used and select <API access>. The Google Map v2 API key is now requested from here. Click on <Create new Android key> in the lower section of the screen.

A new window is opened, wherein you need to enter the generated SHA-1 fingerprint along with the package name that is used for this project.

The package name of the sample project is:

com.greendog.androidstudio.getmebacktomyfirstlocation

We assume that our SHA-1 fingerprint would be: 8B:43:BC:74:04:DD:63:AE:7A: 84:20:98:E1:2D:0B:19:E3:77:9F:3C We need to enter the following in the window: 8B:43:BC: 74:04:DD:63:AE:7A:84:20:98:E1:2D:0B:19:E3:77:9F: 3C;com.greendog.androidstudio.getmebacktomyfirstlocation

and then click on <create>.

The API Access page is then updated and contains a section called "Key for Android apps (with certificates)". The API key is specified in the first row. Copy it and later add it to the AndroidManifest.xml file of the Android project.

Simple API Access

Use API keys to identify your project when you do not need to access user data. Learn more

```
Key for Android apps (with certificates)
API key         AIzaSyBtCMBCKqPZ9HXKaelllgC5QJPmqKYBRGY
Android apps    42:CF:9A:93:83:FC:1A:16:93:45:7D:7E:K3:92:6C:23:44:99:C3:5F:com.greend
                og.androidstudio.gwithebackitchyfirstindation
Activated on    Sep 23, 2013 2:27 AM
Activated by    janebabra@gmail.com - you
```

Key for browser apps (with referers)
API key   AIzaSyBKEGKAxXljlQcyAHveJgMcypemJKYFUY
Referers   Any referer allowed
Activated on   Aug 8, 2013 1:03 AM
Activated by   janebabra@gmail.com - you

Key for server apps (with IP locking)
API key   AIzaSyCVPtGHxmpJqweCCuV4cniN47kcdAfm3r8
IPs   Any IP allowed
Activated on   Aug 8, 2013 1:03 AM

Creating a new Android Map project

You can create a Map project by using the Blank template or the new Google Map template.

Then continue the project creation process using the usual method and complete it.

Open the SDK Manager and make sure that the Google Play Service is installed.

Editing the Gradle file

Then open the *build.gradle* file and add an entry for the Google Play Service:

Add the entry for the Google Play Service under *dependencies*:

```
dependencies {
compile 'com.android.support:support-v4:18.0.0'
compile 'com.android.support:appcompat-v7:18.0.0'
compile 'com.google.android.gms:play-services:3.1.36'
}
```

Editing the AndroidManifest file

First open the *AndroidManifest.xml* file and edit it:

Add the following paragraph and enter your API key in the

android:value="your-key-here" row.

```
<meta-data
android:name="com.google.android.maps.v2.API_KEY"
android:value="your_key_here" />
```
Add another section:

```
<permission
android:name="your.package.name.permission.MAPS_RECEIVE"
android:protectionLevel="signature" /> <uses-permission
android:name="your.package.name.permission.MAPS_RECEIVE"/>
```

and enter the your **package name** accordingly.

In addition, various uses-permissions related to the Internet access and localisation are required.

```
<uses-permission android:name="android.permission.INTERNET" />
<uses-permission android:name="android.permission.ACCESS_NETWORK_STATE" />
<uses-permission android:name="android.permission.WRITE_EXTERNAL_STORAGE" />
<uses-permission
android:name="com.google.android.providers.gsf.permission.READ_GSERVICES" />
<uses-permission android:name="android.permission.ACCESS_COARSE_LOCATION" />
<uses-permission android:name="android.permission.ACCESS_FINE_LOCATION" />
```

Finally, add the entry for using OpenGL ES Version 2 in the AndroidManifest file.

```
<uses-feature        android:glEsVersion="0x00020000"
android:required="true"/>
```

Inserting a map in the app

Add a map using a MapFragment as shown the code snippet of the *activity_main.xml* file.

```
<fragment
    android:layout_width="wrap_content"
    android:layout_height="wrap_content"
    android:name="com.google.android.gms.maps.SupportMapFragment"
    android:id="@+id/map"
    android:layout_below="@+id/title"
    android:layout_alignLeft="@+id/title"
    android:layout_alignParentRight="true"
    android:layout_above="@+id/update_button"
    map:cameraTilt="45" />
```

The **map:cameraTilt="45" entry**

was used here to display a compass on the map. The compass is displayed only when "tilt" or "bearing" is greater than zero. "Tilt" indicates the angle of the camera with the map and "bearing" indicates the alignment.

The button provided below the map was designed using the start_pos.xml file that is stored in drawable/. If you edit this file, you will realise one of the new capabilities of the editor.

Wherever a colour is defined in the row, the edge of the row shows a small square with this colour. If you click on the coloured square, the "Choose colour" window is displayed. You need not open any additional graphics program to get the colour codes. You simply need to click on your desired colour in the "Choose colour" window and done. Java file

If you want to display only one map, you need not edit the MainActivity.java file. In this example, suitable code has been added, e.g. to save the current position, to set a market, to display a compass, to add the "current position icon" and to establish communication with the button.

The compass was activated with

```
mMap.getUiSettings().setCompassEnabled(true);
```

The current position icon was activated with

```
mMap.setMyLocationEnabled(true);
```
Links related to Google Maps and Google Play Service are added at the end of this book.

Using the Google Map template

Since Android Studio Version 0.5.4, a new template called **Google Maps Activity** is available.

The template can be selected as the first activity when creating the project or can even be selected as the second or additional activity later in the project.

The 'minimum SDK' version 9 is required to be able to use this template.

With the first activity, you could have build the GetMeBacktoMyFirstLocation project instead of using the Blank activity template.

The new Map template has some selection options to configure a few settings relevant for Google MAP. It can be modified like other templates and adapted as per your requirements. At least the following 3 entries must be added to the template:

1. Lat Long coordinates

The *MapsActivity.java* file already contains an entry for coordinates; these are however currently set to zero such that the map section is approximately located in the vicinity of Africa.

```
private void setUpMap() {
 mMap.addMarker(new
 MarkerOptions().position(new LatLng(0, 0)).title("Marker"));
    }
```

The LatLng(0,0) entry should be modified to display the desired map section.

2. API key

Similar to the last project, we will again require a 'Google Map v2 API key' that needs to be entered in the AndroidManifest.xml file.

3. GL

We also need to add the entry for the application of GL in the AndroidManifest.xml file:

```
<uses-feature
        android:glEsVersion="0x00020000"
        android:required="true"/>
```

SAMPLE PROJECT

Since we already have an app, whose first activity is a Map Activity, the new example deals with adding a Map Activity with the new Google Maps template in an existing app.

The following is used as the sample project: MyImageSwipeViewer

The project has 2 activities at present:

MainActivity Starts the app

SwipeActivity It is started using the MainAcivity button and shows the slide show

The app idea involves providing an option from the Swipe Activity such that a map can be displayed, wherein the position of the grave from the Bronze Era is provided with a separate marker.

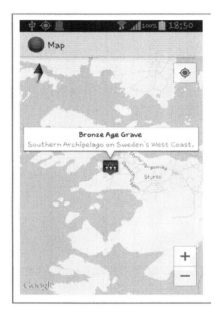

Download the **MyImageSwipeViewer** project from here and then open it in Android Studio:

https://github.com/janebabra/MySwipeImageViewerProject

Creating the new activity using the Google Maps template

Right-click on the package name New -> Google and select the Google Maps Activity template. Assign the names for the Java file and the layout file.

Modifying the entries in the *MapsActivity.java* file

As already mentioned above, we at least need to enter the coordinates for the desired location.

How do we determine the LatLng coordinates of a particular location?

You can search for the address in Google Maps, then right-click on the location in the map and select "What's here?". A small window containing the coordinates is then displayed. Enter these in the *MapsActivity.java* file.

```
private void setUpMap() {
 mMap.addMarker(new
 MarkerOptions().position(new LatLng(57.616029, 11.763617)).title("Marker"));
    }
```

The before mentioned code sets a red, balloon-shaped marker as shown below:

If you want to use a customised icon as a marker, you will need a suitable image. I have found a page on the Internet that provides thousands of icons for Google Maps:

http://mapicons.nicolasmollet.com/markers/tourism/cult-religion/cemetary/?custom_color=402c15

From this page, I have downloaded the following icon, named it *cemetary.jpg* and copied it in the drawable/ folder. We will now add it to the Java code.

The ActionBar is extended with a "MAP" entry

- Create a new *slide.xml* menu file in the menu/ folder and provide it with the following entry:

```xml
<menu xmlns:android="http://schemas.android.com/apk/res/android">
    <item android:id="@+id/action_map"
        android:title="@string/action_map"
        android:orderInCategory="100"
        android:showAsAction="ifRoom" />
</menu>
```

- Add an entry for the name in the strings.xml file:<string name="action_map">Map</string>

- The *SlideActivity.java* file contains the call of the map

```java
@Override
    public boolean onCreateOptionsMenu(Menu menu) {
  // Inflate the menu; this adds items to the action bar if it is present.
        getMenuInflater().inflate(R.menu.slide, menu);
        return true;
    }
    @Override
    public boolean onOptionsItemSelected(MenuItem item) {
        int id = item.getItemId();
        if(id == R.id.action_map) {
            Intent i = new Intent(this,MapsActivity.class);
            startActivity(i);
            return true;
        }
        return super.onOptionsItemSelected(item);
    }
```

Zoom such that the map can be called from the SlideActivity and shows the desired location with a customised icon.

If you wish, you can further improve the look of the map by specifying a zoom factor and changing the viewing angle of the camera using the Tilt option.

The following section is added to the MapsActivity for the camera setting:

```
public final void animateCamera(CameraUpdate cameraUpdate) {
      mMap.animateCamera(cameraUpdate);
// Construct a CameraPosition focusing on the Bronze Age Grave
// and animate the camera to that position.
      CameraPosition cameraPosition = new CameraPosition.Builder()
              .target(grave)
// Sets the center of the map to the Bronze Age Grave
              .zoom(13)
// Sets the zoom
              .bearing(90)
// Sets the orientation of the camera to east
              .tilt(45)
// Sets the tilt of the camera to 30 degrees
              .build();
// Creates a CameraPosition from the builder

mMap.animateCamera(CameraUpdateFactory.newCameraPosition(cameraPosition));
```

The extended project can be downloaded from GitHub:

https://github.com/janebabra/GoogleMapsTemplate

With Google Maps, we can really do a lot of things. Listing all options is naturally beyond the scope of this book.

However, I have given a few links that are worth visiting:

https://developers.google.com/maps/documentation/android/marker

https://developers.google.com/maps/documentation/android/views

https://developers.google.com/maps/documentation/directions/?hl=en

Combining the Android SDK with external SDKs

The Android SDK integrated into Android Studio enables manufacturer-independent app development. The app development does not differentiate whether the telephone/tablet is Nexus, Samsung, Kindle or Sony Ericsson. Additional SDKs (libraries) of specific manufacturers need not be installed. In case of Samsung and Sony Ericsson, you have to work with the manufacturer's proprietary SDKs only if you want to use specific properties that have been exclusively developed by these manufacturers. The best example is There are a few exceptions:

Wearables

Kindle tablets

Samsung devices

WEARABLES

At present, the Android SDK does not have any special classes to develop for "Android smartwatches" (wearables). The three manufacturers of such "wearables" that I know provide their proprietary SDKs in the form of .jar libraries. These SDKs are treated in Android Studio like any other library by copying it to the libs/ folder and adding an entry in the build.gradle file. According to Google, an SDK for WEARABLES will be shortly integrated into the Android SDK. If you are interested in this topic, browse through the sites of Android wearables manufacturers:

Samsung gear

http://developer.samsung.com/samsung-gear

Sony Ericsson Smartwatch

http://developer.sonymobile.com/

Pebble watch

https://developer.getpebble.com/

KINDLE TABLETS

Apps developed using the Android SDK also run on Kindle tablets by default. If you want to use special properties of a Kindle tablet in your app development, you will need the SDK provided by Amazon.

http://kdk.amazon.com/gp/public/gateway

SAMSUNG TELEPHONES AND TABLETS

The principle applicable for Kindle applies here as well. Samsung has a series of advancements that go much beyond the Android SDK.

http://developer.samsung.com/samsung-mobile-sdk

Android Wear

As mentioned, Google has issued the first version of the new **Android Wear SDK** in April.

Android Wear is an SDK for developing the apps for "smartwatches". The version issued at present includes a preview that can be downloaded only by developers who participate in the Android Wear Preview Programme (free).

The Android Wear SDK can be integrated into Eclipse as well as Android Studio. I will however handle only the part that is relevant for Android Studio.

Even if Android Wear is not yet installed, you can view in the SDK Manager that the Android SDK was updates and contains an emulator for Android Wear Smartwatches.

At present, the emulator is the only option to test an Android Wear app since smartwatches with Android Wear were not available in the market before.

Google is working with several hardware manufacturers who want to introduce new smartwatches with Android Wear on the market. These manufacturers include Asus, HTC, LG, Motorola and Samsung.

Motorola and LG have already presented their prototypes in public and have notified that the initial watches will be introduced in summer.

Preview for Moto 360

In order to participate in the "Android Wear Developer Preview" programme, you need to open an account.

http://developer.android.com/wear/preview/signup.html

- Wait for the email -

The reply email contains a link from which the app for the telephone/tablet can be downloaded. The app is required to be able to connect with the Android Wear device (currently only the emulator). In addition, the email also has a link to a zip file containing the support library (Android Wear SDK) and samples.

The Android Wear Preview app

Unfortunately, the Android Wear Preview app can be installed only on devices with Android 4.3 or higher and it is not compatible with the emulator.

The zip file

Examples

In the meanwhile, you can learn about new APIs.

http://developer.android.com/wear/preview/start.html

Installation of the Android Wear system image

- Start the SDK Manager
- Under Android 4.4.2, select the **Android Wear ARM EABI v7a system image**
- Click on **Install packages**
- Click on "Accept the license" and **Install**

Setting up the Android Wear emulator

Start the AVD Manager

- Click on **New**
- Enter either "AndroidWearSquare" or "AndroidWearRound" as the *AVD Name* depending on whether you want to set up a square or a round version.
- As *Device*, select either **Android Wear Square** or **Android Wear Round**.
- As *Target*, select at least **Android 4.4.2 - API Level 19**
- For *CPU/ABI*, select **Android Wear ARM (armeabi-v7a)**.
- As *Skin*, select either **AndroidWearSquare** or **AndroidWearRound**.
- Leave the remaining as it is and click on **OK**. Although **Hardware keyboard present** is not applicable for smartwatches, it must be retained.

Now select the emulator, which we have just configured, in the list of the AVD Manager and click on **Start**.

Then click on **Launch**.

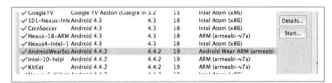

The Android Wear emulator starts and it looks as shown in the following two

figures:

Before you can test the "Wearable Notification" app provided in samples, you must connect the telephone and the Android Wear emulator via the *Android Wear Preview* app.

Setting up the Android Wear Preview app

After installing the *Android Wear Preview* app on a telephone or a tablet, open it:

You should see a message indicating that the app is not yet activated as a "notification listener".

Click on the message to open System Settings. Then select Android Wear Preview and enable the permission.

Now connect the telephone or tablet with the computer via USB. No other Android device may be connected.

The Android Wear emulator should now run and look as shown above.

Then open a Terminal window by navigating to the `platform-tools/` directory of the Android SDK using the cd command.

Enter the following command.

```
adb –d forward tcp:5601 tcp:5601
```

Important:

You must enter this command whenever you reconnect the device via USB.

Back to the Android Wear Preview app.

The app should now show that it has been connected with the emulator.

The Android Wear emulator should indicate that it is connected with a device and show a "g" icon instead of the struck-through Device icon.

The Android Wear emulator now displays the incoming notifications of the telephone.

Adding the support library to the project

The Android Wear Preview support library contains several APIs for optimising the notifications.

The support library named **wearable-preview-support.jar** is provided in the zip file that we have downloaded.

We will need a `libs/` folder to add the library to the project. If you have not created it in the project, create it first. Then copy **wearable-preview-support.jar** to this folder.

We will first add an entry for the support library in the `build.gradle` file:

```
dependencies {
    compile "com.android.support:support-v4:18.0.+"
    compile files('../libs/wearable-preview-support.jar')
}
```

Then click on the "Sync Project with Gradle Files" icon in the toolbar.

The setup process is now completed. You can now test samples or begin with your own projects.

The following link gives suggestions for the "Wearable Notifications" example.

Creating Notifications for Android Wear:

http://developer.android.com/training/wearables/notifications/creating.html

Preparing the app for the Android market

GOOGLE DEVELOPER AND OTHER ACCOUNTS

If you wish to publish your in Google Play, you need to set up a Developer account and pay a one-time fee of $25.

https://support.google.com/googleplay/android-developer/answer/113468?hl=en

If you want to publish in other markets, you will need an account for the respective market.

Android apps are special because you can publish your app even on private servers or Open Source servers such as GitHub, Bitbucket and Google Code. And the best part is you do not have to pay for it.

ADDING GOOGLE ADS TO AN APP

You will need a Google Adsense/ Admob account to add Google's Admob ads to an app.

For this, visit:

http://www.google.com/ads/admob/

Once you log into your Adsense/ Admob account successfully, you can use the "Monitize a new a app" option for the app to add a new project in Adsense.

You can define various configurations such as form and colour. I have selected the Banner format in this example. The size of the banner is determined later in the app. Interstitial can also be used as an alternative to the banner. In this case, the entire screen is filled with an HTML Ad.

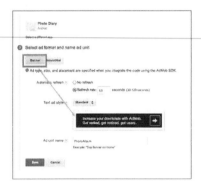

The **Ad unit ID** appears in the last screen to configure the new Admob Ad. It is required later in the app so that it can be added to the app.

AndroidManifest

Internet authorisations must be added to AndroidManifest:

```
<uses-permission android:name="android.permission.ACCESS_NETWORK_STATE"/>
<uses-permission android:name="android.permission.INTERNET"/>
<uses-permission android:name="android.permission.ACCESS_FINE_LOCATION">
```
And the Admob data for this app:

```
<activity android:name="com.google.ads.AdActivity"
android:configChanges="keyboard|keyboardHidden|orientation|screenLayout|
uiMode|screenSize|smallestScreenSize">
</activity>
<meta-data android:value="ca-app-pub-5523788489069928/4148191603"
android:name="ADMOB_PUBLISHER_ID"/>
```

Adding AdView to the layout

An area for Ads must be reserved in the layout in order to make them visible. Adding an AdView is the easiest form. In this example, the banner is added to the Photo Diary app.

An AdView must be added to the layout(s) where Ads need to be displayed. The banner should be displayed in the album as shown in the following figure.

The following is added to the layout_view.xml layout file:

```xml
<?xml version="1.0" encoding="utf-8"?>
<LinearLayout
xmlns:android="http://schemas.android.com/apk/res/android"
xmlns:ads="http://schemas.android.com/apk/lib/com.google.ads"
android:layout_width="match_parent"        android:layout_height="wrap_content"
android:background="@drawable/bg"        android:orientation="vertical">
<Button
android:id="@+id/newbutton"
android:layout_width="fill_parent"
android:layout_height="wrap_content"
android:drawableLeft="@android:drawable/ic_menu_camera"
android:text="@string/neuesFoto"
android:gravity="fill"
android:onClick="newPhoto">
</Button>
<ListView
android:layout_width="wrap_content"
android:layout_height="380dp"
android:id="@+id/main_listview">
</ListView>
<LinearLayout
android:layout_width="match_parent"
android:layout_height="wrap_content"
android:layout_gravity="bottom">
<com.google.ads.AdView
android:id="@+id/adView"
android:layout_width="wrap_content"
android:layout_height="51dp"
ads:adUnitId="ca-app-pub-5523788489069928/4148191603"
ads:adSize="SMART_BANNER"
ads:loadAdOnCreate="true" />  </LinearLayout> </LinearLayout>
```

You will need screenshots before publishing the app in Android markets.

It works the best if you have developed the app for device types, namely telephones as well as tablets.

The easiest option is to use the "Android DDMS" in Android Studio.

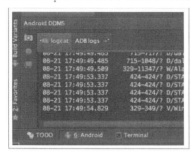

For this, you need to run the app either on an emulator or an Android device connected via USB.

Then click on the camera icon in the top-left corner of "Android DDMS".

As shown in the last image, different settings can be configured here. Selecting different screen sizes might be the most important one.

The same on a tablet

SIGNING

In the menu, click on "Build" and then on "Generate Signed APK".

The "Generate SignedAPKWizard" window then opens

You can either load an existing key or create a new one. After making your choice and filling all fields, there is one last stop. If Proguard needs to be used, you need to select the checkbox for "Run ProGuard" and navigate to the configuration file to load it. Now click on <Finish>.

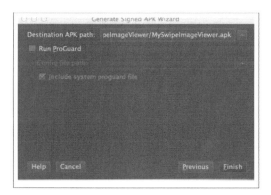

If everything is OK, the success message is shown in a small window. Click on "Reveal in Finder" to navigate to the signed MySwipeImageViwer.apk. This APK is ready for uploading in one of the Android markets such as Google Play.

ProGuard

What is Proguard?

Proguard is a free programming tool to edit Java files in compiled status, i.e. class and jar files. Proguards capabilities include:

- Compressing (shrinker)
- Optimising (optimiser)
- Making decompilation difficult (obfuscator)

Proguard is often used to prevent the theft of the program code. If a protection such as Proguard is not used, a finished app (APK) can be opened with special decompilation programs. The package name can be changed and the "new app" can be sold under a different name. App in which Proguard was used can still be opened using a decompilation program. But it is decrypted by Proguard, class file are renamed, etc. and hence using this source code is extremely difficult. The time required to convert this "Proguard code salad" into a separate new app is probably the same as that required for creating an app from scratch.

Using Proguard

Android Studio already has the in-built option of using Proguard in an app. Proguard can be exclusively used in conjunction with the creation of a release APK.

If an app is signed using the aforementioned wizard, you simply need to select the checkbox in front of "Run ProGuard".   For the subsequently described signing via Gradle, runProguard **false** is changed to runProguard **true in the build.gradle file of the project.**

```
buildTypes {

    release {

        runProguard true

        proguardFiles getDefaultProguardFile('proguard-android.txt'), 'proguard-rules.txt'

    }

}
```

SIGNING A RELEASE APK WITH GRADLE

When you use the Signing wizard, an Info message is shown. For Android Studio 0.5.1, it is as follows:

Google has already changed this message several times, but the wizard functions as described at the beginning.

There are 3 options to create the configuration for a release APK with Gradle.

1. Option:

All information is entered in the *build.gradle* file:

```
        android {
...    signingConfigs {
release {
storeFile file("release.keystore")
storePassword "******"
keyAlias "******"
keyPassword "******"
}   }
buildTypes {
release {
signingConfig signingConfigs.release
}   } }
```

2. Option

The password is not entered in the plain text format in the file, but it needs to be entered for all inputs:

```
signingConfigs {
    release {
        storeFile file(System.console().readLine(" Enter keystore path: "))
        storePassword System.console().readLine(" Enter keystore password: ")
        keyAlias System.console().readLine(" Enter key alias: ")
        keyPassword System.console().readLine(" Enter key password: ")
    }
}
```

3. Option

In the third variant, an external file such as the ~/.gradle/gradle.properties file is used to store all information.

```
RELEASE_STORE_FILE={path to your keystore}
RELEASE_STORE_PASSWORD=*****
RELEASE_KEY_ALIAS=*****
RELEASE_KEY_PASSWORD=*****
```

Only references are specified in the build.gradle file:

```
...
signingConfigs {
    release {
        storeFile file(RELEASE_STORE_FILE)
        storePassword RELEASE_STORE_PASSWORD
        keyAlias RELEASE_KEY_ALIAS
        keyPassword RELEASE_KEY_PASSWORD
    }
}
```

```
buildTypes {
    release {
        signingConfig signingConfigs.release
    }
}
....
```

Irrespective of the option selected, the call for creating the release APK is triggered using the following command in the Terminal window from the project directory.

```
gradle assembleRelease
```

Appendix

What is the Gradle build system?

Gradle is a Java-based build management automation tool
Google integrated Gradle in Android Studio using a newly developed Gradle plugin for Android Studio. Android Studio downloads Gradle 1.7 when creating an Android project for the first time. Therefore, the creation of the first project requires slightly more time depending on your Internet connection.

In Android Studio, the "Gradle build system" is the chosen build system. Gradle replaces "Ant" that is used in Eclipse. "Old Eclipse" projects must be converted from Ant to Gradle before they can be imported in Android Studio.

One of the most important features of the "Gradle build system" is that it allows creating different versions of the same app: e.g. free and paid apps using the same code.

Gradle is primarily controlled by a script called "build.gradle". This script is written in "Groovy DSL"; it is easy to read and write.

Build scripts can be really small if the project is based on the default structure for projects. An example is given below:

```
buildscript {
repositories {
mavenCentral()
}
dependencies {
classpath 'com.android.tools:gradlexx'
}
apply plugin: 'android'
```

The Buildscript {} element is actually required only by the script.
The actual content is "apply plugin: 'android'".
This script generates as fully runnable "unsigned apk".

Which Gradle file is responsible for my Android project?

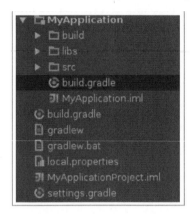

The responsible Gradle file is stored in the root directory of the project.

Normally only the build.gradle file needs to be edited for an individual project. In case of multiple projects, an entry must be added in the settings.gradle file (see the Sherlock ActionBar).

What is the structure of a build.gradle script?

Android Studio provides a standard build.gradle file for every newly created project. If the project needs to be further developed after creating, the Gradle file must be modified.

For the "My Application" example, Android Studio has generated the following build.gradle file:

```
buildscript {
    repositories {
        mavenCentral()
    }
    dependencies {
        classpath 'com.android.tools.build:gradle:0.5.+'
    }
}
apply plugin: 'android'

repositories {
    mavenCentral()
}

dependencies {
    compile 'com.android.support:support-v4:13.0.+'
}

android {
    compileSdkVersion 17
    buildToolsVersion "17.0.0"

    defaultConfig {
        minSdkVersion 8
        targetSdkVersion 16
    }
}
```

How does Gradle find files for external dependencies?

Gradle searches them in a "repository". A repository is actually only a collection of files that are organised as per the group, name and version. Gradle understands different repository formats such as Maven and Ivy, and provides various options to access the repository, e.g. using the local file system or HTTP.

Android Studio defines the central Maven repository for Gradle by default:

repositories {
    mavenCentral()
    }

Android Studio has an integrated Gradle plugin that is required for working with Gradle. These dependencies are included in the Gradle file as follows.

dependencies {
    classpath 'com.android.tools.build:gradle:0.5.+'
    }

This information indicates an Android application.

    apply plugin: 'android'

If you want to create a library instead, you need to select "apply plugin: 'android-library'".

The default template that is used for creating a new project has already integrated the android-support-v4 library.

```
dependencies {
compile 'com.android.support:support-v4:13.0.+'
}
```

This information is derived from decisions that were made when creating the project.

```
android {
compileSdkVersion 17
buildToolsVersion "17.0.0"
defaultConfig {
minSdkVersion 8
targetSdkVersion 16
}
buildToolsVersion "17.0.0"
defaultConfig {
minSdkVersion 8
targetSdkVersion 16
}
}
```

The Gradle script can be divided into 3 main areas:

1. buildscript {... }
  It configures the building of the control code.

2. The 'android' plugin provides all aids required for testing and building the applications. If a library is used for the project, the entry must be 'android-library'.

3. android { ... }
  This part is the entry point for the Android DSL. All parameters for the Android build are configured here. It is required only for the compilation target by default. In this example, "compileSdkVersion 17" is used for this purpose.

Is it necessary to edit the build.gradle file in all projects?

No; if your project no longer uses external libraries other than support-v4, which is already integrated, there is no need to edit the build.gradle file.
  Some examples where you need to edit the default build.gradle file:
  - When using the Sherlock ActionBar
  - When using Admob
  - When using test projects
  - For multi-app projects

For editing the Gradle file, double-click on the build.gradle file to open it in the editor and edit it.

Using Gradle from the IDE or from the command line

Select "Build" or "Run" in the menu to create the project from the Android Studio IDE.

Open a Terminal window and navigate to the project folder to use Gradle from the command line.

Example:

Assume that the AndroidStudioProjects folder is the folder in which all Android Studio projects are saved.

After creating the "My Application" sample project, we should see a new folder called "MyApplicationProject" in the AndroidStudioProjects folder. This folder has the "gradlew" command in the form of gradlew.bat for Windows and gradlew for Unix-based systems such as Linux and Mac OS X. This Gradle wrapper should be used for the command line.

The Android plugin contains 6 "anchor tasks":
    assemble

The task to assemble the output(s) of the project
    check

The task to run all the checks.
    connectedCheck

Runs checks that requires a connected device or emulator. They will run on all connected devices in parallel.
    deviceCheck

Runs checks using APIs to connect to remote devices. This is used on CI servers.
    build

This task does both assemble and check
    clean

This task cleans the output of the project

These can be called from the command line using the following command:
    gradlew tasks

To view a complete list and dependencies between tasks, enter:
   gradlew tasks --all

Integrating libraries

   Libraries are available in different versions:
   Individual Java file / jar file, example: support-v4:13.0
   Java library project directory: Example: Sherlock ActionBar

Integrating a "remote jar" library

In the sample project, the android-support-v4 library was automatically integrated. It is comes from the Maven repository. Therefore, 2 entries were required to integrate the library.

The first entry is
   repositories {
   mavenCentral()

to define the valid repository from which the following library should be retrieved.

The second entry is
   dependencies {
   compile 'com.android.support:support-v4:13.0.+'

It specifies which library from the Maven repository should be integrated into the app.

This procedure is also applicable for other libraries if they need to be retrieved from a remote repository. The library need not be copied to the libs/ directory.

```
dependencies {
    compile 'com.android.support:support-v4:18.0.0'
}
```

Integrating a local library

The local library must be located in a project directory. You first need to create a libs/ directory at the level of the src/ directory and copy the desired library in it.

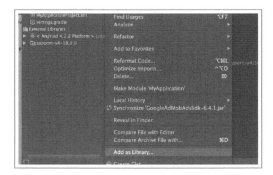

Right-click the file in the libs/ folder and select "Add as Library".
Add the following in the build.gradle file:

compile files('libs/android-support-v4.jar')

Example - integrating GoogleAdMobAdsSdk

Download GoogleAdMobAdsSdk-6.4.1.jar from
https://developers.google.com/mobile-ads-sdk/download
and copy/drag the unpacked jar file in the libs/ folder.

Right-click the file in the libs/ folder and select "Add as Library" (Global).

Open the build.gradle file in the project folder and add the following entry:
**dependencies { compile files('libs/android-support-v4.jar','libs/
GoogleAdMobAdsSdk-6.4.1.jar') }**

In the menu, select Build → Rebuild Project

Admob can now be imported and used; the location, where the Ad should appear,
needs to be specified using a Java file or the layout file and "uses-permission" and
AdActiviy and Admob ID for the app must be added to the AndroidManifest.xml file.

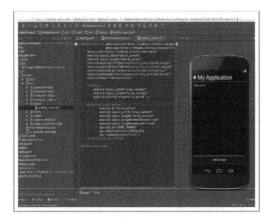

Example for 2: Sherlock ActionBar

Download the latest and Gradle-compatible version of the Sherlock ActionBar files from git clone git://github.com/JakeWharton/ActionBarSherlock.git

Drag the resultant directory in the project such that it is at the same level as that of MyApplication.

Then open the settings.gradle file and add the following for the Sherlock ActionBar:
include ':MyApplication', ':ActionBarSherlock:actionbarsherlock'

Open the build.gradle file in the Sherlock ActionBar directory and add

the following:
dependencies { compile project(':ActionBarSherlock:actionbarsherlock') }

This procedure is only a temporary solution. The complete release should integrate a project library as an ".aar" file that is comparable with the integration of ".jar" files. As soon as this functions, the chapter is updated.

GameEngines with Android Studio

This chapter deals with both Open Source game engines, namely AndEngine and libGDX

AndEngine

Preparing the AndEngine library

Download the library and import it in Eclipsehttps://github.com/nicolasgramlich/AndEngine

In Eclipse, export the AndEngine project (without the AndroidManifest.xml file) File -> Export -> Java -> JAR file

Save as, e.g. **AndEngine.jar**

Start a new project in Android Studio and name it, e.g. "TowerOfHanoi" for the example discussed here. Name the activity "TowerOfHanoiActivity.java". Assign the same name to both xml files since a fragment layout is not required. Create a libs/ folder in the root directory of the project and copy the AndEngine.jar file into it. Open the project structure under Libraries + Button > java > and search the jar. Link the jar library with the project.

Open the *build.gradle* file and then add the code for the jar library:

    dependencies {

    compile files('libs/android-support-v4.jar')

    compile files('libs/AndEngine.jar')

    AndEngine is now ready for use

Visit the following links to download samples for AndEngine.

https://github.com/nicolasgramlich/AndEngineExampleshttps://github.com/janebabra/TowerofHanoiProject

LIBGDX GAME ENGINE

Creating the project structure

You must download the following file for the setup:

http://libgdx.badlogicgames.com/nightlies/dist/gdx-setup-ui.jar

First create a folder for storing the game files.

Copy the gdx-setup-ui.jar file, which we have just downloaded, into this folder.

Double-click the setup file, or, if this does not function, enter the following command on the command line:

    java -jar gdx-setup-ui.jar

Click on Create.

From section 1, we only require "Generate the desktop project".

In section 2, click on the selected icon to download the libGDX library.

Section 3 should thus look as shown in the screenshot.

In section 4, click on "Open the generation screen" and then on "Launch". It then builds the required project structure.

Once the "All done" message is displayed, you can close the window.

Now is the time to import the project in Android Studio. Select Import Project from the Welcome screen and import the entire folder.

Accept the suggestions and click on Next until you reach **Libraries – Library contents**. Rename the 3 libraries such that their name corresponds to their contents as shown in the following figures. This is required to ensure that libraries are maintained in a better manner with respect to each other as far as the module configuration is concerned.

Continue with Next and Finish.

Module configuration

Right-click on the first folder in the project structure and select "Open Module Settings".

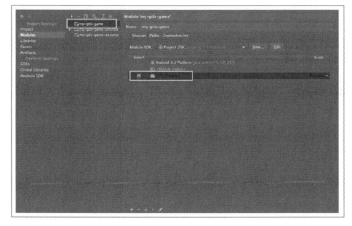

Click on libGDX Shared for Export.

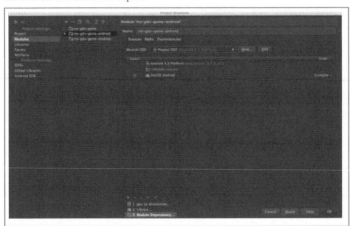

Select the **Android module from the modules and click on the** + button to add a
"Module Dependency".

Select the main module (my-gdx-game) from the list and confirm with OK. The result should look like the following.

Repeat this process for the desktop module.

Editing "run configuration" for Android

Enable "Show chooser dialog" under "Target Device".

Editing the "desktop run configuration"

Click on the + button in the top-left corner and select "Application". Then assign a name to the configuration.

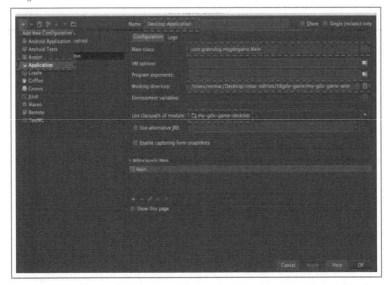

Select **Main class**.

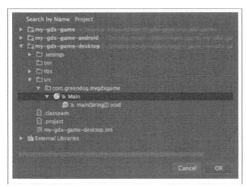

Set the "Working directory" to the "assets" directory of the Android configuration.

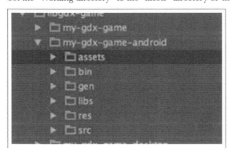

The Classpath receives the path of the desktop module.

Run the desktop version

Run the Android version

The configuration is now complete.

You can use this configuration to develop the desktop and Android versions of a game, run and test them and, last but not the least, can create an APK. However, this configuration does not include the Gradle build system. You can manage without it. However, if you think that a Gradle project structure is required, you must add it manually. It is also the first attempt of a Gradle setup. Unfortunately, it did not function during my test. Here is the link of the Gradle-libGDX project on GitHub. I am sure there will be further developments in this regard in future. https://github.com/libgdx/libgdx-gradle-template

Using Version Control (VCS)

Android Studio allows working with the following VCS:

Git, GitHub, Mercurial and Subversion.

You must install the corresponding program on your computer in order to use one of the systems For Git and GitHub, it would be "git", for Mercurial "hg" and for Subversion "svn".

CONFIGURING THE VCS FOR THE CURRENT PROJECT

Step 1: Configuration of the VCS

From the Welcome screen -> Project Defaults -> Settings -> Version Control

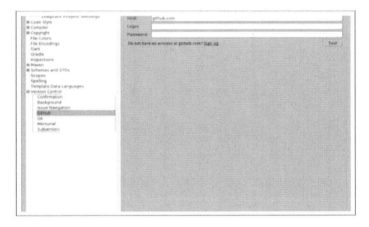

Setting up GitHub

In order to connect the project with GitHub, you must first open a GitHub account; for this, click on "Sign up" in the GitHub window. In the configuration, enter the desired email and the password that you need to use for opening the GitHub account.

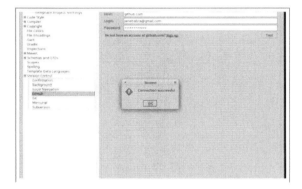

To ensure that the connection functions, click on the Test button and wait for the success message.

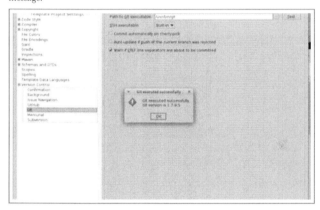

Step 2: Activate the VCS in the current project

In order to activate the current project for working with a VCS, select the "VCS" from the menu bar and then select "Enable Project for Version Control Integration".

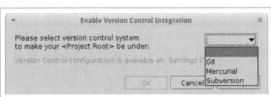

Enable Version Control Integration

Please select version control system
to make your <Project Root> be under:

Git
Mercurial
Subversion

OK   Cancel

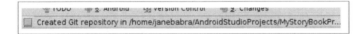

Created Git repository in /home/janebabra/AndroidStudioProjects/MyStoryBookPr...

Now the menu offers all options related to the VCS, e.g. "Share project on GitHub"

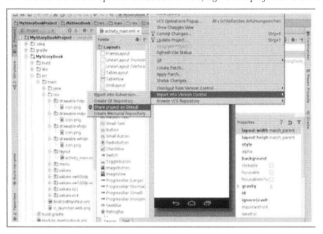

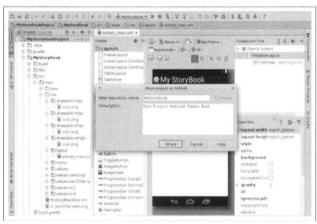

or adding patches, etc

Product Flavours - Build Types - Build Variants

One of the objectives to use Gradle in Android Studio to provide the programmers with an option to create different apps using the same app code.

This becomes possible by defining the so-called Flavors.

Main areas of usage of Flavors:

Creating different versions of the same app, e.g. a free and a paid version.

Packing the app differently so that it can be uploaded as a multi-apk to the Google Play Store.

The combination of 1 and 2.

When the app contains Flavors, it must use the same API.

You can create Flavors by creating a separate directory structure for Flavors and adding an entry for the "productFlavors DSL container" in the build.gradle file.

The following example creates an app that contains both **production** and **testing** Flavors.

These Flavors differ in

- App icon -> drawable-xxxx

- App name -> strings.xml

- Background colour -> activity_main.xml

- Displayed contents -> Constants.java

A new project with a blank template is created for this purpose.

Our next task is to build the project structure for Flavors. This must be manually created in the Project structure window.
You need to start with creating two sub-directories bearing the names of Flavors in the **src/** directory. Then create all resources required for individual Flavors under these directories.

The complete structure for this project should look as follows:

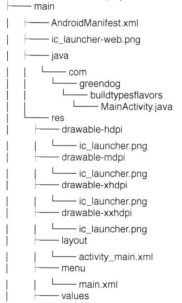

```
├──── main
|    ├────── AndroidManifest.xml
|    ├────── ic_launcher-web.png
|    ├────── java
|    |    └──── com
|    |         └──── greendog
|    |              └──── buildtypesflavors
|    |                   └──── MainActivity.java
|    └──── res
|         ├────── drawable-hdpi
|         |    └──── ic_launcher.png
|         ├────── drawable-mdpi
|         |    └──── ic_launcher.png
|         ├────── drawable-xhdpi
|         |    └──── ic_launcher.png
|         ├────── drawable-xxhdpi
|         |    └──── ic_launcher.png
|         ├────── layout
|         |    └──── activity_main.xml
|         ├────── menu
|         |    └──── main.xml
|         ├────── values
```

```
|     |     ├─── dimens.xml
|     |     ├─── strings.xml
|     |     └─── styles.xml
|     ├─── values-v11
|     |     └─── styles.xml
|     ├─── values-v14
|     |     └─── styles.xml
├─── production
|     └─── java
|           └─── com
|                 └─── greendog
|                       └─── buildtypesflavors
|                             └─── Constants.java
└─── testing
      ├─── java
      |     └─── com
      |           └─── greendog
      |                 └─── buildtypesflavors
      |                       └─── Constants.java
      └─── res
            ├─── drawable-hdpi
            |     └─── ic_launcher.png
            ├─── drawable-mdpi
            |     └─── ic_launcher.png
            ├─── drawable-xhdpi
            |     └─── ic_launcher.png
            ├─── drawable-xxhdpi
            |     └─── ic_launcher.png
            └─── values
                  └─── string.xml
```

Then open the build.gradle file and add the following entry:

```
productFlavors {
    production {
        packageName "com.greendog.buildtypesflavors"
    }
    testing {
        packageName "com.greendog.buildtypesflavors.staging"
    }
}
}
```

Important:

The names for Flavors (production and testing) must match the directory structure. MainActivities should not be different, e.g. one in the main/ directory and other in one of the Flavor folders. Varying contents are provided in another Java file which is Constants.java in this case.

Contents of the Constans.java file for the production Flavor:

package com.greendog.buildtypesflavors;
public class Constants {
public final static String BASE_URL = "https://github.com/janebabra?
tab=repositories";
}

Contents of the Constans.java file for the testing Flavor:

package com.greendog.buildtypesflavors;
public class Constants {
public final static String BASE_URL = "https://github.com/janebabra/
MySwipeImageViewerProject/blob/master/README.md";
}

This is slightly different for resource files; the same file name is possible in Flavors and in the main/ folder, e.g. strings.xml.

The concept of Gradle allows defining build types as well as product Flavors for a project. The combination of build types and product Flavors then results in build variants.

For this example, 4 build variants are possible:
ProductionDebug
ProductionRelease
TestingDebug
TestingRelease

Building the build variants from the IDE

Click on the <Build Variants> button on the left side of the IDE to open the Build variants window.

You can select individual build variants from the Drop-Down menu under the Build variant. Then click on <Run> if you want to run the selected variant on a telephone or an emulator.

This method functions only for the debug variants.

If you want to test a release variant, you need to add the entry for the release key in the build.gradle file.
 Example:

```
android {
        signingConfigs {
        production {
              storeFile file("other.keystore")
               storePassword "android"
               keyAlias "androiddebugkey"
               keyPassword "android"
           }
        }
```

Building different build variants from the command line

If the product Flavors have been defined, extend the assemble command:

assemble<Variant Name>

assemble<Build Type Name>

assemble<Product Flavor Name>

gradlew assemble

Examples:

gradlew assemble	Builds all 4 variants
gradlew assembleDebug	Builds ProductionDebug and TestingDebug
gradlew assembleRelease	Builds ProductionRelease and TestingRelease
gradlew assembleProductionDebug	Builds only ProductionDebug
gradlew assembleProduction Builds	ProductionDebug and ProductionRelease

The source code for this project is available on GitHub:
https://github.com/janebabra/BuildTypesFlavorsProject

Links

Some resources for learning Java

http://www-cs-faculty.stanford.edu/~eroberts/books/ArtAndScienceOfJava/
http://www.greenteapress.com/thinkapjava/html/index.html
http://www.mindviewinc.com/TIJ4/CodeInstructions.html

Android & Android Studio
Where does one get help inside and outside Android Studio?

Inside Android Studio
From the Help menu and from "Tip of the Day".

Outside Android Studio
Android Tools Project Site
Provides information about changes in new versions, **Release Status**
    http://tools.android.com/overview

SDK Manager

    http://developer.android.com/sdk/exploring.html

AVD emulator
    http://developer.android.com/tools/devices/emulator.html
    http://developer.android.com/tools/devices/emulator.html#acceleration

Android Developers Blog
    http://android-developers.blogspot.se/2013/05/android-studio-ide-built-for-android.html

Welcome to Google Developers Live
    Learning from others and putting a lot of time and energy into it
    https://developers.google.com/live/

The app example for Android Studio from I/O Google
    https://github.com/bradabrams/stopwatchio13
    Detailed explanation for examples
    http://bradabrams.com/2013/06/google-io-2013-demo-android-studio-cloud-endpoints-synchronized-stopwatch-demo/
    The original version of the Ultimate Stopwatch app (Eclipse)
    https://code.google.com/p/android-ultimatestopwatch/

Overview of Google Cloud Endpoints
https://developers.google.com/appengine/docs/java/endpoints/

Google Cloud Console
https://cloud.google.com/console

Google API console,
https://code.google.com/apis/console

Google Cloud Messaging for Android Docu
http://developer.android.com/google/gcm/index.html

Issue Tracker
https://code.google.com/p/android/issues/list

Google's GIT Repository for Android Studio
https://android.googlesource.com/platform/tools/adt/idea/

Gradle Plugin User Guide
http://tools.android.com/tech-docs/new-build-system/user-guide

User Guide from gradle.org
http://www.gradle.org/docs/current/userguide/userguide.html

Multiple APK Support
http://developer.android.com/google/play/publishing/multiple-apks.html

Build Server and Test Server
AppThwack
https://appthwack.com/
TestDroid
http://testdroid.com/
instrumentTest example
https://www.manymo.com/pages/blog/android-testing-in-the-cloud
Manymo
https://www.manymo.com
Travis
https://travis-ci.org/

Google Map API v2

https://developers.google.com/maps/documentation/android/
http://developer.android.com/google/play-services/maps.html

Google Play Service SDK

http://developer.android.com/google/play-services/index.html

Code samples on Google Drive

http://goo.gl/AhurvS

Original Web address:

**https://drive.google.com/file/d/0B69hr4dMQB_RYUNNQU5yT1JMTUk/edit?
usp=sharing**

You may also find something useful on the following Github:

https://github.com/janebabra?tab=repositories

Imprint

Texts: © Copyright by Barbara Hohensee
Barbara Hohensee
Utlandagatan 33
41261 Göteburg
Sweden
greendogdevelop@gmail.com
All rights reserved.

Date of publication: 8 April

Blog for this book:
http://google-android-studio.bogspot.com

Author: Barbara Hohensee

Printed in Great Britain
by Amazon.co.uk, Ltd.,
Marston Gate.